SPLAS...

FUN IDEAS FOR USE WITH UNDER-FIVES

Christine Orme and Christine Wood

Scripture Union
130 City Road, London EC1V 2NJ

©1992 Christine Orme and Christine Wood

First published 1992
British Library CIP Data
A catalogue record for this book is available from the British Library

ISBN 0 86201 742 4

Permission to photocopy
The Allabout sheets (on pages 71-93) and all artwork are copyright free
and no permission is needed to photocopy them.

Cover design, book design and artwork by Tony Cantale Graphics

Printed and bound in Great Britain by
Ebenezer Baylis and Son Ltd, The Trinity Press, Worcester and London.

CONTENTS

INTRODUCTION

ABOUT THIS BOOK

Chaos reigns: Matthew and Gemma are having a fight over Matthew's teddy; Vincent is quietly dismantling the very beautiful flower arrangement done in memory of Mrs Bloggs – and his mother hasn't noticed yet! Sarah is wailing loudly that she doesn't like it and she wants to go home; three toddlers have set up base camp behind the communion table. Timothy is insisting on telling you (**very** loudly in your left ear) all about the party he went to yesterday (that's today's theme), and to cap it all your own child has suddenly become very protective of you, and is wrapped round your neck like an octopus, and shoving hard with his spare hand any other child who has the temerity to come near you…Does this seem familiar? Read on!

In recent years it has been exciting to see many different sorts of church-based groups springing up to cater for parents and young children. In a largely non church-attending society, such midweek groups often represent a church's most significant area of outreach. Their potential influence is enormous.

We know, from observation and from our own experience, that many of these groups are set up and run by mothers occupied with their own pre-schoolers or by clergy busy with other duties and with little or no experience of under-fives. Neither may have the time or the energy to start from scratch in preparing material. This book is written for everyone who is already involved with under-fives and for those wondering whether they should – or could – be! We hope it will give you a vision of the joy of working with small children and lots of practical help and ideas to know where to begin.

The book is divided into three sections: the first has general information on the needs of pre-schoolers and their carers, how to set up the right kind of group, and how to do the singing, praying, storytelling, craft work etc that such a group may need.

The central section of the book consists of forty topics with suggestions for craft activities, songs and rhymes to fit in with a Bible link. These topics are grouped into seven 'series'.

We have deliberately not set out all the topic outlines in any particular format as we want the book to be a resource for all kinds of groups, including 'pram services'. Each topic has a suggested Bible link with a focus for children and another for adults, several activity/craft ideas, and a list of songs and rhymes, some from easily available books, others new to this one. Many of the songs can also be used as games with under-fives. We hope you will be able to select material relevant to your particular group, without feeling tied down to a particular format.

The final section is a series of photocopiable sheets, one for each topic, with ideas about further activities for adults and children to do at home together. These are most suitable for three, four and five year olds.

The appendix lists useful addresses and additional information.

One final word of explanation: we are aware that not all families today consist of mum (at home) married to dad (at work) and their two children. Many children come from single parent families or 'reconstituted' family goups where only one adult may be the biological parent. Many mothers work and pre-schoolers are often cared for by childminders or relatives other than their parents. References in the text to mums/parents should therefore be taken to include adult carers of any description. We live too in a multi-ethnic society so please try to reflect this in, for example, pictures you use in presenting our material.

We hope you and the members of your group have as much fun using the book as we have had compiling it.

YOUNG CHILDREN AND THEIR FAMILIES

SPIRITUAL DEVELOPMENT IN YOUNG CHILDREN

■ PARENTS' NEEDS

We can safely assume that mothers of young children will have certain things in common. Many will feel permanently tired from the exhausting demands – physical and emotional – of small children. Some will feel confused about aspects of child-rearing despite, or even because of, the amount of advice available today. Others may be suffering from post-natal depression in varying degrees, and many will be just plain lonely. This may all sound a bit negative, but it's easy to underestimate the adjustments new parents must make.

The experience of parenthood can highlight spiritual needs too: the Christian parent may find that freedom to be involved in church life as much as previously (or even simply time to read the Bible) is severely curtailed. Non-Christians may find the responsibility of a new life triggers a search for spiritual values. A church-based group can help both – the Christian, by providing contacts with other Christians in similar circumstances, and the non-Christian, who may well look to 'the church', and in particular its representatives in the group, for guidance on bringing children up in the Christian faith.

Young/inexperienced parents may hope a group will provide:
• reassurance that they're 'doing all right',
• a break from caring,
• some adult contacts and company,
• an opportunity to talk,
• a chance to worship with their children (in a pram service group) especially if this is not possible on Sundays.

Such groups can offer useful practical 'models' of parenting; young parents separated from all but their immediate families and those whose own experiences of family life were inadequate may learn from seeing good adult-child interactions and skilled handling of behaviour problems. On another level they may gain ideas about the choice of playthings and equipment. In addition, although the tide is slowly turning, it's still generally true to say that in the UK at least, young children are not welcomed in public places. (Compare for example the number of young children in restaurants – apart from fast food outlets – with the number seen eating out on the Continent.) It's good therefore to provide a place to which adults and young children can go together, where they can 'be themselves' without adults apologising!

Of course many groups will encounter more complex needs, spiritual, emotional and material, and will need to find appropriate ways of handling them, but whatever form a midweek group takes, it should aim to cater for the needs listed above. They are very obvious and basic, but it's easy to lose sight of them in our thinking and planning.

Young children can and do enjoy a relationship with God. Throughout the Bible we are made aware that fellowship with God is dependent not on a particular level of intellectual understanding but on a childlike faith and trust. Spiritual truth is 'spiritually discerned' (1 Corinthians 2:14 NIV) whatever our age. Many of us fall into the trap of thinking that knowing something 'in our heads' – intellectually – is the same as knowing it 'in our hearts' – spiritually. So, a three year old can understand that God loves him, just as a ninety-three year old can, but – and it's a very big 'but' – the three year old's **response** will be appropriate to his age.

■ BIBLICAL GUIDELINES

Old Testament
We read in the Old Testament that parents were responsible for passing on to children the truths of their faith, and it seems this was done in ordinary family conversation (eg Deuteronomy 11:18-21). At times 'visual aids' were used to stimulate questions, as in the institution of the Passover, Exodus 12:25-27, and in Joshua 4:20-24. Besides this, the whole religious life of the Jews was enriched with symbols which could, and doubtless often did, prompt children's questions.

New Testament
The New Testament indicates that even unborn children can be spiritually aware; if we look at the story of Mary's visit to her cousin Elisabeth (Luke 1:39-45) we see that Elisabeth, prompted by the Holy Spirit, declares that the child within her 'leaped for joy' at Mary's greeting. We must assume from this that very young, even unborn, children can be spiritually sensitive.

Jesus' own teaching
The gospels give us other glimpses of the special place children have in God's heart. On at least three occasions Jesus refers to the significance of children; when women brought babes-in arms to him he said the kingdom of God belongs to 'such as these', and the only way to enter or receive that kingdom was 'as a little child' (see Matthew 19:13-15, Mark 10:13-16, Luke 18:15-17).

In Matthew 18:1-6, Jesus speaks forcefully about little children, pointing out that we need their childlike humility and trust, and that acceptance of them is acceptance of him. He warns against 'despising' or 'offending' them and suggests in verse 10 that they all have angels. Jesus' words give us a very clear basis for the setting up of church-based groups for under-fives!

■ CONCLUSIONS

So how do children develop spiritually? Perhaps we need to answer this question in two parts, firstly how do children learn 'ideas' about God – and what we might call 'doctrine' or 'Bible/Christian knowledge' – and secondly, how do they absorb that knowledge so that it becomes part of them? The first – learning about God, Jesus, the Bible, and learning hymns and songs, is what we might call 'intellectual' knowledge – what they know with their minds. The second is 'spiritual' knowledge – what they understand with their spirits and emotions – and is really far more important!

Let's consider the first aspect: the Bible seems to assume that children will ask questions, particularly if stimulated, and we know that once a child has grasped the idea of asking questions – a few stages on from learning to talk – there's no stopping him! Most of these questions will arise from something the child has seen, heard or experienced.

Children will at some stage, having grasped the general idea of 'cause and effect', begin asking about the natural world: Who made the trees? What makes flowers smell so nice? and so on. The answers they receive, and their own interpretation of those answers, help to shape their ideas about the world and their place in it. I still remember looking up at the stars as a small child, and asking 'Who put the stars in the sky?' The answer ('God did') was interpreted by my four-year-old mind in terms of my own limited experience (of gummed paper stars kept in a tin) and so to this day I have a most unscientific mental picture of God taking the stars out of a tin box at night and putting them in place!

Since questions tend to be responses to different stimuli, the child from a Christian or church-attending home is perhaps more likely to ask questions about 'spiritual' things because she will be exposed to a greater number of 'religious' stimuli, and will therefore have more to fuel her questions. She will attend church, and maybe an age-related teaching group; without conscious effort she will learn hymns and songs, not all of them specifically for children. She may also pick up some set responses and prayers, acquiring some 'faith terminology' without understanding much at an intellectual level, at this stage. All the time, small children in church will be absorbing the atmosphere of worship, prayer and praise, and will, given the right environment, grow gradually into a deeper understanding of God's truth, and a personal commitment.

At home, children of Christian families will be used to private or family prayers as well as church ones. These children will probably be used to saying a simple grace before meals, and will be familiar with several Bible stories by the age of about two and a half. At this stage some may even begin to grasp that Jesus is a special person: one day Helen, aged two and a bit, got Plasticine in her hair – the old-style Plasticine which was virtually irremoveable from clothes, carpets – and hair. In vain I tried everything I could think of to remove the offending Plasticine, and finally said in desperation, 'It's no good; Mummy will have to cut your hair.' The response was immediate: 'Mummy ask Jesus; Jesus get it out.' Regrettably, my faith was not up to hers, but it was an interesting insight into that child's spiritual development: she had understood that Jesus was special, and at two and a bit had applied that knowledge to a problem situation. This was by no means an isolated incident, and one of the joys of Christian parenthood is to see children beginning to grasp at their own level the truths of the Christian faith.

Children from 'non-religious' homes will have fewer spiritual stimuli, though all children ask questions of the 'Who made ...?' variety. Even children whose parents aren't churchgoers may experience a church event that triggers questions – a wedding or baptism for example, while a sad experience such as the death of a grandparent, or even a pet, will almost certainly do so. We can pray that their children's questions will start adults in our groups searching for answers.

We need to bear in mind, too, that many people, without the benefit of a Christian home or regular churchgoing, have had an awareness of God for as long as they can remember. Our spiritual development – as children and adults – is **always** a response to God's work in our lives and not something started by us. This should encourage those working with groups from largely unchurched backgrounds.

Turning to the second – and more important – aspect of 'how children develop spiritually', we need to consider how children 'internalise' what they hear about God and Jesus, ie how they apply it to themselves (quite unconsciously of course as pre-schoolers) and make it part of them.

Children interpret what they are told about the physical world in the light of their own experience; the same is true of their interpretation of what they are told about spiritual things. The key factor here is relationships. Christianity, uniquely, teaches that we are able to enter into a family relationship with God as our Father, and Jesus his Son as our elder brother (Hebrews 2:11), and that the Church is the family of God, so all Christians are brothers and sisters. This is wonderful! – so long as your experience of family life and of parents is good, warm and healthy. In a very real way parents 'are' God to their young children. Quite apart from the fact that small children think that parents/primary carers know everything and can do anything, it is that relationship, good or bad, which colours the child's interpretation of the facts she is taught about God.

The child from an unhappy home or the child who is the victim of abuse – physical or mental – will find it almost impossible to 'internalise' the idea that God is a Father. Warm, caring relationships nurture a child's growth in faith; inadequate or bad ones hinder it. We need to be aware that not all the children in our groups will feel good about God as a Father.

FOSTERING SPIRITUAL GROWTH IN YOUNG CHILDREN

So much for theory! How is this relevant to work with young children and families? Where do we start? Firstly, we need consciously to acknowledge each child's individual worth before God. We need to pray for an increasing spiritual awareness in each one, and for great sensitivity in all those who help with the group. Even children from homes where parenting is inadequate or bad can be helped to understand God's unconditional love and acceptance if they receive it themselves from other caring adults. Their parents, too, may benefit from seeing how others relate to children.

Secondly we need to accept that before the age of about two and a half there will be little response to **words** about God, though children from about 18 months will often join in songs. This does not mean 'anything will do' for under-threes! It won't! Even babies are sensitive to atmosphere and the key factor with under-threes is a warm and happy one. Children (and adults) attending a group like this are likely later on to grow into an awareness of God.

When thinking about fostering spiritual growth in three to five year olds, we need to remember that children of this age, although they use the same language as adults, actually think very differently. They cannot understand abstract ideas so take everything absolutely literally. When talking to them we must beware of using, for example, figurative language which could be misinterpreted. Listening to a child's questions and comments often shows us the stage he has reached – as well as being an excellent way of building up relationships and showing we care for them as individuals!

Such questions and comments are most likely to arise when adults and children are doing things together. Activities such as those in this book have value not just because children 'learn through play' but because such play activity sessions where adults get alongside children can provide a stimulating yet relaxed environment in which children feel able to talk and ask questions. By getting alongside in this way the adult 'affirms' the child's value as an individual, demonstrating to him that he is worth spending time with.

So how do we avoid the pitfalls? Where do we begin? When God wanted to show us what he was like he sent Jesus. That's one good way for us to begin too. Simply told stories of Jesus can lay the foundations for a mature adult faith. We can also use children's natural interest in our world as a starting point to talk to them about our loving Creator God. Above all we need to remember that the way we treat small children is far more telling than anything we say. Relationships matter more than words, especially at this stage.

The apostle Paul reminds us that 'faith comes from hearing the message' (Romans 10:17) and that it doesn't matter who 'plants' and who 'waters' since it is God who gives growth (1 Corinthians 3:5-9). Working with under-fives is a 'planting' situation so don't be discouraged if you don't see obvious results. We live in an 'instant' culture and need to remind ourselves that God is never in a hurry and he will work out his purposes in and for the families in our groups.

SETTING UP A GROUP

How/where do I start?
- **Find a friend.** It's best, especially if you have under-fives yourself, not to try to start anything alone; if you do and your child is unwell, for example, on the day the group meets, you have problems immediately. If possible try to find at least two other people to help you get started.
- **Remember, small is beautiful!** It's better to start with half a dozen mums and toddlers and grow from there, than to aim to cater for too many initially.

Where, when?
- **Decide where you will meet.** Some groups start successfully in a home, but a hall of any size usually lends itself better to a variety of activities. This may involve hire-charges (see the section on finance).
- **When to meet requires careful thought.** Avoid clashing with the local baby clinic, or toddlers' sessions at the swimming pool.
- **Would a morning or afternoon be best?** If a morning, consider starting within half an hour of local infant schools, so that mothers with slightly older children can come straight on after taking children to school. (This saves having to get babies and toddlers dressed up twice.) An afternoon group needs to start early, so that those with older children can leave about 3pm to collect them from school.

Deciding how often to meet is important
- **Once a week** is probably ideal but may put too great a burden on the helpers, especially if the team is small. The advantages are obvious: it becomes a regular event in a small child's life, and if a week is missed it isn't too long till the next time. (This book assumes a group meeting weekly during school terms.)
- **Once a month** seems to be quite a popular choice, especially for pram services, but the disadvantage is that if someone misses one then there's a gap of two months and shy people, especially non-churchgoers, might find it hard to pluck up courage to return.
- **Once a fortnight** would seem a good starting point.

What kind of group?
Three main types of group are *parent and toddler* groups (technically under-threes though in practice many include older children, unless the group runs in conjunction with a playgroup catering for three to five year olds), *playgroups* (which cater almost exclusively for three to five year olds), and *pram services* which will probably have older children as well as the pram and buggy brigade.

All these groups cater for under-fives and their families but the emphasis may be different:
- **A parent and toddler group,** church-based, will probably provide a number of simple supervised activities as well as toys for unsupervised play, and have a few minutes with some sort of spiritual input, usually at the end. This may be geared just to the adults present, or to adults and children.
- **A pram service** is more likely to start with some sort of Bible story or songs, and then move on to activities, play and refreshments, so there may be proportionally more time given to the 'God spot' than there is at a toddler group.
- **A church-based playgroup** will have children without their parents for much of the time, but the whole atmosphere and ethos will, ideally, reflect God's love and concern for the whole family. It is usually considered most beneficial for children to attend a playgroup for at least two or three sessions a week, so, as numbers are strictly controlled by local authorities, a playgroup must of necessity cater for fewer children than groups where the parents stay as well.

Some modern church buildings have enough flexibility for a combination of things: an area for mothers and babies, still within view of their toddlers, and another area where more structured, playgroup-type activities are available for older children.

Parent and toddler groups and pram services offer opportunities for parents and minders to talk to and play with their children, and facilitate the all-important task of building relationships. Many of the activities in this book have this aim in mind and a 'perfect' finished product is not the intention of the craft activities. Some of the more structured activities may not be as suitable as others for playgroups, where the emphasis is on the child's creativity and free expression.

Finance
This needs careful thought. What expenses must you cover (eg hall hire/heating) and what activities do you hope to provide which will need an initial expenditure? Paint and glue, for example, will almost certainly have to be bought in bulk, and you need to work out the cost of refreshments. From these you should be able to estimate a term's or a session's running costs, and set a 'per session' charge per family. It's probably best to charge per adult or per family, because if you charge per child a mother with three children may be deterred from coming – and she may most need it. If you want to keep weekly charges low, but you need a 'kitty' to replace paints etc, a registration fee, paid on the first visit, might be an idea.

Equipment
Think before you buy: what you will need depends on the nature and size of your group and on the storage space available. Lack of lockable storage space can affect insurance premiums. Remember that it may be possible to borrow large items (such as a climbing frame) from other groups. And although many people may be prepared to give equipment (such as old toys) it is important to stress that they must be good quality and safe.

Planning
Try to plan at least half a term in advance as that gives plenty of time to collect materials. Try to get other people involved in the planning

as it's amazing how really good ideas can be sparked off when two or three people plan together. If you want people to make visual aids give them plenty of time and offer to pay for their materials.

Helpers

Before you start, find out exactly how many people are prepared to help on a regular basis. Playgroups must by law have a basic staff of qualified or suitably trained people – NNEB, infant teachers, etc, or those who have done a PPA course, as well as volunteers. (See Appendix, page 95, for details.)Older people may not volunteer, but can often offer very reliable help. Other helpers may have toddlers or babies of their own and therefore be a little restricted in what they can do, so it's good if you can also enlist help from people with children at school. Decide who will be responsible for, say, getting the room ready, buying and bringing refreshments, welcoming people and taking money if you are going to charge, mixing up paints and supervising activities. Obviously you will expect parents to keep an eye on their children, but as a safety measure have an adult helper to watch children using potentially dangerous equipment.

Many toddler groups have a parents' rota for serving coffee, but this isn't necessarily a good idea: the mother with a tray of hot drinks and a toddler clinging to her skirt is an accident waiting to happen, and some people may feel unable to do anything even as straightforward as making coffee in a strange environment. Whatever your system, make a rota and give somebody the job of reminding people of their tasks for the next session.

Layout

Be prepared to try several before you find the most satisfactory for your particular group. Ways must be found to keep crawlers safe from the hazards of older children on push and ride toys and to keep younger toddlers out of the glue and paint.

If you have 'big' equipment (slide, climbing frame, etc) keep it in one area and designate another for quieter activities – books, dressing up, Lego/Duplo. Site paint and glue in the spot where spills will matter least, and near the kitchen for easy mopping up and replenishing of water supplies.

Make sure that people serving or collecting hot drinks can do so without putting children at unnecessary risk.

How will you cater for parents? Chairs in a circle is the usual arrangement, and if you can put 'sitters and crawlers' on a rug in the middle, and other activities outside the circle, so much the better.

If you are holding a pram service you may have less equipment and fewer activities, but you can still be imaginative in the arrangement of the room. If you meet in a church don't be afraid to move the chairs! It's far better to have children sitting on a rug at the front where they can see, hear and participate than perched several rows back in chairs or pews too big for them, with everything going over their heads. For adults too, a traditional church seating arrangement can be unwelcoming, especially to non-churchgoers. If pews are immovably fixed, it might be better to use another room where seating can be arranged more satisfactorily.

Shoe-box library

This can be a very effective way to get people reading Christian books. Select a number of easy-to-read paperbacks with attractive covers which can be stored in a couple of shoe-boxes when not on display. Most popular categories tend to be books about child handling, family life, time-management, as well as autobiography and books by well known authors like Cliff Richard. True stories of families coping with real life problems are also well read. Make sure that books are in good condition – tatty dog-eared ones don't enhance the church's image!

Many people will read a Christian book before they are ready to talk about Christianity, and once people are used to borrowing them you could have a book party (see the section on special events) before Christmas or the summer holidays, and include Christian books for children as well as adults.

Insurance

This is absolutely essential. If you meet in a church building you will almost certainly find that the church's insurance is fully comprehensive for all activities taking place on its premises, but if at any point you might want to organise an outing, check that the insurance covers that too. Otherwise the PPA offers an excellent insurance package – see Appendix for details.

Record keeping

Keep simple records – names, addresses, phone numbers – so that people can be contacted if, for example, there has to be a last minute cancellation.

Record children's birthdays, so that you can send a card from the group and sing 'Happy Birthday' at the session nearest the day. This is very important to children so make as big a fuss as you like!

If funds permit send a card, a posy of flowers or homemade cake when someone has a baby. Little things like this mean a lot.

Other small points

- Think of an easy name and maybe a symbol for your group; that helps people to have a sense of belonging. Have something that you do together each week – sing a special song, hold hands to say the same simple prayer, light a candle.
- If you meet less often than once a week, have a card or sheet with dates and times for the group, and telephone contact numbers.
- Provide nappy-changing facilities as well as a potty for toddlers and a step-stool of some kind if washbasins are at adult height.
- Look out for ideas for activities and displays, or new uses for household packaging. If a local infant school, nursery unit or playgroup has an open day, go along and see what they are doing. Watch TV programmes for under-fives – you'll then know what the children in the group are talking about and you can often pick up ideas.
- Provide a variety of activities, if possible, but never force children to join in, remembering that things apparently innocuous to an adult (like balloons or sock puppets) can be frightening for some small children. It is a mark of our respect for them as individuals to allow them to opt out.

OUTREACH EVENTS

As your group begins to jell you may find that you wish to do something more as a means of bridging the gap between the church and the families in the group who don't attend church. The following suggestions may give you some ideas to work on.

For couples

- An informal supper evening - perhaps in early spring when not much else is going on.
- Do you have anyone in your church who could come and talk informally (and interestingly!) on a topic related to children, particularly in a way that involves parents? Parents will often come to such events, and it helps to establish that God is interested in us as whole people not just as souls with bodies on.
- Book parties are usually popular, especially if you can link them to a theme, eg books for Christmas or Easter, or for the summer holidays. Include refreshments, so that people feel more relaxed, and perhaps get one or two people to recommend books which they have found helpful or which their children have particularly enjoyed.
- In the autumn, a Harvest supper could be a good opportunity to invite parents who don't normally attend church.
- Invite parents to 'parenting' or 'marriage-enrichment' courses.

For families

- Look out for opportunities locally for something a little different. For example, a Christian farmer in a village near us opens his farm to the public one weekend every spring at the height of the lambing season. Something like this is an unforgettable experience, especially for children growing up in an urban environment.
- In the summer an outing to a local beauty spot or open place is always popular.
- A bonfire party around November 5 is worth considering, especially as many people, aware of the hazards of fireworks, prefer to go to an organised display. Hold it early in the evening so that pre-schoolers aren't too tired – say 6.15pm onwards. Remember that young children hate bangs, so stick to pretty fireworks and a few sparklers.

For women

- Many women have leisure interests which they would be pleased to demonstrate to young mums. Is there someone who could do an evening on, say, 'Cooking for Christmas' or 'Christmas decorations to make at home'? Other people might talk about patchwork or painting or photography…ask God to guide you about what to follow up in this area.

It is hoped that this kind of activity will achieve two things – bring people into contact with the church and church members, and establish friendships from which we can talk naturally about our faith.

LET'S BE PRACTICAL

This section is intended to help you with all those details that are so often taken for granted in resource materials, and which you then have to look up elsewhere. If some of it seems to be stating the obvious, it is for the sake of those with absolutely no previous experience at all. And if some of the instructions seem fussy or to involve unnecessary expenditure, that may be because we need to be aware of the underlying message we are communicating to the children and their parents about how important we think they are. A piece of paper creased or carelessly cut to size may imply a 'they won't notice anyway' attitude; a piece of paper which tears easily when little hands are trying to colour on it produces frustration in the child, for whom the 'picture' is very precious.

For special activities you may need to buy a few things – paper doilies, crepe or tissue paper, glitter, straws, paper plates and brass paper fasteners – but this should only involve a small additional outlay for those weeks.

■ HOW TO USE COLOURING

What with?

Chunky crayons are best for the very young, but as their skills improve they prefer the thinner crayons, as they have more control over them. It's best, then, to provide a selection of both, plenty of them, and in as many different colours as possible. See crayons as a short-term item in the equipment box, as they are easily broken, frequently trodden on and soon begin to look unattractive.

Coloured pencils are only suitable for children who have a high degree of co-ordination, and are not recommended for the equipment box.

Felt-tip pens seem an attractive proposition, and certainly the thick-tipped pens are very satisfying to use. The snag here is the ease with which felt tip gets onto clothes, and although washable felts can be bought, Mums are sometimes not impressed if their children are covered in felt-tip pen at the end!

Colouring pre-drawn pictures

In spite of the difficulty little ones have in colouring pre-drawn pictures, there is value in occasionally having a picture for them to colour in. Keep the picture bold and clear, with no unnecessary detail to confuse them, and no smaller than A5 size. If you can't draw there are books available (see 'Resource books' on page 17) with a variety of pictures suitable for photocopying.

■ HOW TO USE CRAFT

The cardinal rule if you work with under-fives is never throw anything away!! Almost anything can be used for **collages**: packets, kitchen roll middles and polystyrene trays can all be used for **junk modelling**; old magazines and catalogues give plenty of scope for montages; plastic containers will grow **seeds**; oddments of wool can be pressed into service to make hair and scraps of material to dress **people** … the list is endless.

Collages

These are abstract pictures made from a variety of materials – old greetings cards, fabric scraps, tissue paper, gummed paper etc, stuck onto card or sugar paper. Do be careful, though, with younger children: beans, dried pasta, milk bottle tops and other similar items may get put into mouths instead of stuck on the paper!

Non-sticky glue sticks are simple to use but expensive, and another alternative is to obtain a washable glue and pour small quantities into shallow containers. Provide the children with paint brushes and two or three can share each pot. It's worth making sure you buy the right kind of glue for what you want to do, as it's very frustrating if things don't stick. 'Paste' or 'gum' will only stick paper to paper. PVA glue, or 'school glue' is washable and will stick paper, card, fabric, wool, foil, beans, pasta, etc but *not* plastic.

You can make a totally abstract collage or you can pick out the theme and make a collage based on it. For instance, a picture of a child, with the words 'God loves me' already printed on could be 'dressed' with pieces of material, and strips of wool for hair.

Montages

A montage is a picture built up of small pieces of torn paper, rather like a mosaic. You begin with a simple line drawing, say a plate with sausages, potatoes and beans on it, done on a large sheet of paper (A3 or larger). The children then tear up tiny pieces of coloured paper – brightly coloured magazines or comics will do – and stick them, mosaic-style, on to the drawing. The more the pieces overlap the better, as the secret is to avoid gaps. If you want the colours to be realistic do some sorting out first and only provide the colours you want. Otherwise just let the children tear and stick as they choose.

Montages make good displays and can be on any theme. Alternatively, very simple drawings could be given to each child to make into a montage for taking home. Many of the suggestions made in this book for collages could also be adapted for montages.

Modelling

Children love to play with modelling materials like Plasticine, playdough or bread dough. They also like to play at 'cooking', so provide plenty of cutters and rolling pins for them to make 'biscuits'.

The most basic playdough is just salt, flour and water, in the proportion one measure of salt to two measures of flour and enough water to bind it to a paste. This has a short life, especially as it dries and hardens if left uncovered, but that can be used to advantage since it can be painted. Cut-out shapes, such as stars, can be threaded on string and decorated when dry to make Christmas tree decorations.

To make a longer lasting playdough take: 1 cup of flour; 1/2 cup of salt; 1 cup of water; 1 tablespoon of cooking oil; 2 teaspoons of cream of tartar; food colouring if desired. Place all the ingredients in a saucepan and stir over a medium heat for about five minutes until it has the consistency of dough. When it has cooled, put it in a plastic bag and keep it in the fridge until required.

This has the consistency of commercial modelling dough and will last a month or more. It also has the advantage of washing off clothes!

■ HOW TO GROW SEEDS AND PLANTS

- Small children are fascinated by things that grow and love having the chance to 'grow their own'. Mustard and cress grow in just a few days and can be sown on cotton wool on polystyrene trays or in yoghurt pots. Egg-shell 'people' can be made by putting damp cotton wool into clean egg-shells and sprinkling with mustard or cress seeds. A face is drawn on the shell with felt-tip pen, and in a few days 'hair' begins to grow as the seeds germinate. This is a very popular activity with little ones, is easy to prepare and carry out, and can link with several themes.
- Another way of using seeds is to sow seeds at home and take the young plants to the group. Easy-to-grow plants such as pansies, marigolds or nasturtiums will reach the potting-on stage in just a few weeks, and can then be planted in compost in yoghurt pots as part of the activities related to the theme.
- Bulbs can be planted in a similar way.
- Pulses are very easy to grow; you can sprout brown lentils, continental lentils, aduki beans etc in jam jars, by rinsing them out in fresh water twice a day and leaving a little in the jar for the pulses to absorb. Broad beans can be sprouted in a jam jar lined with blotting paper. Put the beans between the glass and the paper and you can see the sprouts growing!

■ HOW TO USE COOKING

Making bread
This is another activity very much enjoyed by the twos and upwards – and usually the leaders as well!

Mix your dough no less than three hours before you will want to use it with the children, to give it time to rise for the first time. One bag (1.5kg) of flour will make between 30 and 40 rolls – they don't need to be very big – and two little sachets of yeast will be plenty.

At the start of the group time knead the dough on a floured board and give each child a small piece. They will thoroughly enjoy squeezing and shaping it in their hands. Have some flour available for dusting. You need to have some way of identifying the rolls after they have been baked. One way is to cover the trays with non-stick parchment and write each child's name beside their bread.

If the dough is shaped at the beginning of the session, the rolls will prove during the remainder of the time (a warm place is essential) and can be cooked towards the end. Small rolls take about 30 minutes to prove, 10 minutes to cook in a conventional oven (very hot, 230°C, 450°F, Gas 7–8) and 2–3 minutes in a microwave oven.

Making chapatis
If breadmaking is too difficult to handle with your group, why not try chapatis? They don't require any rising, but you need an open top cooker and plenty of adult help.

For about 16 chapatis you need: 1lb wholemeal flour; 16 cups of water (or milk and water mixed); half a teaspoon salt.

Sift the flour and salt together and gradually add the liquid to make a non-sticky dough. Take small balls of dough and roll them out or shape them with your hands into large thin circles. Heat a dry, non-greased frying pan or griddle until very hot and place the chapatis in it one at a time, cooking them for about 20 seconds only on each side. Remove the chapati from the pan, and place it under a hot grill, where it will puff up rapidly. Stack the chapatis on a plate lined with a clean cloth (otherwise the bottom one sticks) covering them each time to keep them warm and supple. Serve warm with a little butter – perhaps folded into four to make them easier to handle.

Icing biscuits
Plain biscuits, such as Rich Tea or shortcake biscuits can be iced and decorated by young children – with a bit of help! Make up some glace icing in a variety of pastel colours and have available different sorts of cake decorations to sprinkle on the top.

Making peppermints
For this activity you can either buy ready-made fondant icing from a supermarket and flavour it, or make your own. The ready-made variety is very sticky, so you will need plenty of extra icing sugar.

If you make your own, you will need: 1 egg white; about 8oz/225g icing sugar; peppermint flavouring; green food colouring if desired.

Lightly beat the egg white with a fork, then work in enough icing sugar to make a pliable dough. Add the colouring and flavouring before the dough gets too firm.

Give the children a small amount of fondant paste each. They can then roll it out on a surface (sprinkled with icing sugar, to prevent it sticking) and cut it into shapes with tiny cutters. Leave the peppermints to dry on baking trays.

■ USING MUSIC WITH THE UNDER-FIVES

Small children respond naturally to music, especially rhythm. They love to create patterns of sound for themselves and experiment with different kinds of instruments. And most young children like to sing, although many do not develop a reliable sense of pitch until they are older. Any group for the under-fives, then, should have lots of opportunities for singing, playing and responding to music.

Playing to children
If possible, have some music playing at the beginning of your time together, either 'live' or a tape. There are some excellent tapes of songs for children available and the children will pick up many tunes just by hearing them in the background. By choosing your music carefully you can begin to set the scene for the day's theme.

Choosing songs
Many songs written for children have actions accompanying them. These help children to understand and remember the songs, and the very youngest can join in with them even before they can manage the words. You can always make up actions if the songs don't already have them; it's not difficult, and great fun!

Playing instruments

Playing simple musical instruments to accompany the songs is also an enjoyable activity. Percussion instruments can be purchased from toy shops or music stores.

If you want to make your own 'shakers', instructions for making simple percussion instruments are given later in this section. You can involve the children in this activity. We haven't included suggestions on percussion in every outline, for reasons of space, but any song which isn't already an 'activity song' may have percussion accompaniment. Not all accompaniment needs to be noisy: even young children can learn to play their instruments softly, and they can be very effective in a quiet song.

Finally, don't be afraid to sing the same songs over and over again, week after week. Children love repetition – it reassures them and helps them to learn. If you can find a song to be your 'theme tune' so much the better. Singing it at the beginning will establish a routine for the children and help them to realise that the group time has begun.

One other important point to remember is not to introduce too many new songs at a time. One a week is too many. Let one song become a favourite for a while before introducing another.

One simple way of introducing a new song, especially if the words are slightly complicated, is to play it while the children accompany it with simple instruments. That way, they become familiar with the tune, hear someone singing it, and later learn the words quite easily.

Musical games

These are fun to play and help the children to develop listening and copying skills.

- **Pass on a clapping rhythm:** Sit in a circle with the children and clap a very simple rhythm (eg to the word 'Peter'). The children then each copy it in turn.
- **How many ways can you play a tambourine?** Sit the children in a circle and give one of them a tambourine. Ask them to play it any way they like, but it has to be different from the person who has just played it! (They can pat it with their hand, tap it on their head, or hit it on the floor).
- **Change a rhythm**: The leader claps a simple rhythm (eg to the word 'saus-a-ges'). The children copy the rhythm in turn, but in a different way from the person before them. So the person following the leader may copy the rhythm by stamping their feet, slapping their thighs, tapping their head etc. If this is too difficult for your group, an alternative game is to ask the children to suggest how the rhythm could be copied, and then all doing it together.
- **Play some instruments**: Give each child a percussion instrument. Say a phrase which has a simple rhythm, like 'Jesus loves me' or 'sausages and chips', and ask the children to copy it with their instruments. When they know what to do, try listening to each group of instruments in turn, to find out how differently they sound.

How to make musical instruments

- **Shakers**: Collect old plastic bottles with their tops and soak off their labels. Let the children stick decorations on the bottles. Help them to partly fill the bottles with sand, pasta or dried beans. Screw on the tops securely and then wrap sticky tape round the tops to prevent little fingers from unscrewing them and

experimenting with the contents (such as pushing peas up noses or choking on pasta!).
- **Bells**: Buy several small wooden spoons and let the children decorate them with stickers, felt pens or paints. Using coloured ribbons, help them to tie on small bells. Secure the ribbon with some glue, wrap it round the spoon handle several times and tie it securely, so that the bells can't be removed. (A spot of glue, or nail varnish, on the knot makes it difficult to untie.)

■ RESOURCES

A list of music books we have used in the outlines, together with their abbreviations, is on page 20. Here is a list of some other music books and tapes we have found useful with the under-fives.

Books

A & C Black publish a variety of song books suitable for children of all ages, including:
Alleluya! (thoughtful songs)
Apusskidu (favourite songs – pop, noisy and jolly)
Mango Spice (Caribbean songs).

Other useful song books for children are:
Come Follow! The Fisherfolk (Mel Bay Publishing Inc., ISBN 0 87166 106 3) and accompanying tape (CT 2042)
Good Morning Jesus (Palm Tree, ISBN 0 86208 048 7)
The Rainbow Song Book (Word Music – songs of praise for the threes to tens)
Songbook for the Troops (Kingsway, ISBN 0 86065 833 3)

Tapes

Come Follow! The Fisherfolk (CT 2042)
Family Praise Favourites, Ishmael (SFC 144)
Ishmael's Praise Party (Vols 1&2 – SFC 201; Vol 3 – SFC 220)
Junior Praise (eight tapes available – Marshall Pickering Records)
Kid's Praise (eight tapes available – Maranatha Music and Tapes)
Songs for Little Troopers, Ishmael (SFC 212)

■ HOW TO PRESENT STORIES

Children love stories. You can **read** them, **tell** them, **dramatise** them, use **pictures** or **flannel graph**s to illustrate them, or use **puppets**.

Before we look at *how* to present a story, the question needs to be asked, 'Do we have to use a Bible story?' The answer is 'Not if it's not relevant.' If you decide against a Bible story, there may be another book which relates to your theme, so don't be afraid to use it instead. Let the children see that the church isn't separate from their world and that God is just as interested in Postman Pat as they are!

Reading stories

Provided that it has plenty of bright, bold pictures to look at, small children respond well to having a book read to them. There is an art to it, though. First you need to learn to read upside down, so that the children can see the pictures as you read. If you find that impossible, an alternative is to develop the art of reading with the book somewhere in the vicinity of your ear, so that while you hold it up for the children to see you are able to cast a surreptitious glance at the text to see what comes next. Don't forget that you also need to have as much eye-contact with the children as possible while you read.

If you find the stories are too long for the children to sustain concentration you may prefer to 'talk the pictures', just drawing out the relevant information. It is important to decide how you are going to use the book *before* you read it to the children, but be aware how attentive the children are and alter your style if necessary. If you feel they are getting restless, try asking them questions about the pictures or commenting on the action: 'What do you think this man is doing?' (point) or 'What do you think Jesus is going to do next?'

Don't be afraid to use 'secular' children's stories too, if they are appropriate to the theme. So if you are thinking about the wind, use *Mrs Mopple's Washing Day* as well as Mark's account of the storm on the lake, or even instead of it. By planning your sessions thematically, you can present the same things in lots of different ways.

Telling stories

In spite of our telly-orientated world, a story well told still holds us enthralled. Children, especially, respond to the eye-contact a 'told' story encourages and, in some intuitive way, respond emotionally as you invite them into the world you are creating with your words, your face, your body. Don't be afraid to become fully involved: use your face, especially your eyes, to show feelings; make your body big or small, according to the character you are portraying; use the whole range of your voice; use your hands, too, if you can, to indicate size or height.

Drama

Acting out Bible stories is a good way of bringing them to life for small children. You can keep props to a minimum and no special clothes are necessary nor any skilled acting. All that is needed is to create the characters and tell the story from their point of view. There are several ways of using drama with little ones.

- Stories with a small number of major characters can be acted by adults. A variation on this is to have one person telling the story and the other miming the characters.
- Involving the children in acting can be great fun for them and for the helpers. They enjoy being crowds following Jesus, sitting by the lake watching the miraculous feeding of the 5000, being disciples, etc. Involve them in their feelings: 'Haven't we walked a long way with Jesus today? Are your feet feeling tired?' or, 'The boat's tossing about an awful lot, I'm beginning to feel scared. Are you? I wish Jesus would wake up.'
- A variation on this is to suggest that the children all take on the character you are talking about: for instance, if you are telling the story of Moses, the children could first all be his mother, rocking him to sleep; then Miriam, hiding in the bulrushes keeping watch; then the Princess, being surprised at finding a baby in the water, taking him out and cuddling him.

However you decide to include the children, it needs to be carefully thought out beforehand. On the whole, it's better not to single children out, unless you know your children and your group *very* well.

Pictures

These don't have to be complicated or elaborately drawn to be effective: in fact the simpler they are, the better. Make sure that the pictures are big enough and bold enough for all the children to see clearly, and if you put any writing on them do use lower case letters and not CAPITALS. If you have the use of an OHP you can draw or trace any sort of picture on to acetate sheets and show them as you tell the story. If you can't draw, see the resources list below for helpful books which have illustrations you can copy.

Flannel boards

A very old idea, this, but still useful, especially with younger children, who are fascinated by pictures apparently sticking to nothing! To make one, cover a board with old blanketing or a piece of brushed nylon sheet. To make pictures stick to the board, back them with more blanketing or brushed nylon. You can attach a small piece of Velcro to them, which sticks well, but the figures have a longer life if you back them.

As you introduce each character, place the figure on the board, and move the figures about as you tell the story.

Puppets

What do you imagine when you think of puppets? Postman Pat, Camberwick Green, Sooty, Andy Pandy, Punch and Judy? All very sophisticated puppets, worked by professionals. But anything will serve as a puppet: wooden spoons, empty wool cones, dolls, teddies, hand puppets – the list is a long one.
Poseable dolls are easy to use. So are stuffed toys, of any variety: young children seem to have no difficulty relating to a teddy dressed up as Simon Peter!

- Wooden spoons can have faces painted on them and be 'dressed' in oddments of material. Spoons are useful as two different faces can be drawn on either side and the spoon turned around as necessary – think of Mary in the garden on the morning of the resurrection, for instance.
- If you know someone with a knitting machine, ask them to save you the insides of their cones of wool. The cone itself can be covered with material, and a head made from Plasticine, papier maché or even a small balloon, fixed on to the top.
- Hand puppets are simple to use. You can make your own using a paper bag or a piece of scrap material. Draw a face on an oval of card and stick it to the outside of a small matchbox. Put your hand inside the bag, or drape the material round it, and push two fingers into the matchbox. (Your other fingers can be used as 'arms'.)
- Providing a 'stage' for the puppets needn't be a problem, either. A large cardboard box with a square cut out of its side will serve as a theatre. Even a table or a couple of chairs covered with a blanket will do, provided the 'puppeteers' aren't too obvious.

■ HOW TO USE AN OVERHEAD PROJECTOR

An overhead projector (OHP) can be used in a variety of ways:
- The words of hymns and songs can be displayed clearly.
- OHPs can be used effectively for story telling. You can prepare the acetates beforehand, each acetate having part of the story on it. As you lay one sheet on top of another, the drawings show through, so you can add bits as you go along, ending up with a complete picture.

- And did you know it is possible to photocopy pictures on to acetates? Make sure that you purchase the acetates specially produced for photocopying, though – ordinary acetates will melt in the copier.

   One word of warning about copying, however: if you want to use words or pictures from published material you may be in breach of copyright, so it's wise to check first.
- If you want very large pictures, say for a wall display, it is possible to project from an OHP directly on to paper fixed to the wall. You can then draw round the enlarged projected image.
- One or two safety aspects need to be borne in mind. *Do* make sure that no one can trip over the wires – where possible, feed them under carpets. *Do* watch out for little Johnny, just learning to stand up, who is likely to use the table, the leads or anything else available to haul himself up. *Do* remember that little ones will explore anything, including electrical sockets. *Don't* leave the OHP on unattended, the bright lights are very attractive to young children. *Don't* move any OHP while it is still hot.
- *Use Your Overhead* by Lee Green (Victor Books, ISBN 0 88207 467 9) is a useful book with lots of ideas for using OHPs.

■ STORY AND RESOURCE BOOKS

The books listed here are good resources for Bible stories – simple text, bright illustrations – or deal with the world of the under-fives in a sensitive way.

Bible stories

The Lion Book of Bible Stories and Prayers – A selection of Bible stories illustrated with line drawings and photographs – compiled by Mary Batchelor (Lion Publishing, ISBN 0 85648 239 0)

Little Fish Books are very small books, ideal for little people. There are three series, with eight books in each series: *About Jesus; About You and Me; About Bible People* (Scripture Union).

The Lost Sheep; The Two Sons; The Precious Pearl; The House on the Rock – Simple text and bold illustrations – four books by Nick Butterworth and Mick Inkpen (Marshall Pickering)

Palm Tree Books – a series of books telling Bible stories in a straightforward way, with brightly coloured cartoon-type illustrations. There are over thirty titles available from Palm Tree Press.

The Palm Tree Bible – simple text, and illustrations similar to other Palm Tree books. The Old and New Testaments are published separately by Palm Tree Press. ISBNs 0 86208 103 3 (OT) and 0 86208 122 X (NT).

Story books

Books in the series Little Lions Under Fives, and Little Lions New Experiences are ideal books for experiences which a small child may find slightly worrying. Titles include *Me…At the Dentist; Me…In Hospital; Me…At the Swimming Pool; Me….At the Zoo; Gran's Grave; Moving House; The New School; The Wedding*. Published by Lion Publishing.

Resource books

Instant Art (Palm Tree Press). There are several books in this series, giving copyright-free line drawings, cartoons and other artwork for church groups to duplicate for their own use. The perfect answer for those of us who can't draw very well!

Help, I Can't Draw is a series of four books (published by Kingsway) of copyright-free illustrations.

■ PRAYING WITH UNDER-FIVES

Prayer with the under-fives is a long way from quiet times with eyes shut and hands together! And, we are inclined to say, so it should be!

   Prayer, at any age, is an encounter with the living God, sharing thoughts, feelings, hopes, fears – simply being in his presence and absorbing his life. So in enabling little ones to pray we begin with where they are: with their world, their limitations in terms of concentration, and their 'blooming, buzzing confusion' about who God and Jesus are. Prayer becomes active and visual, as well as quiet: sometimes involving gluing or colouring, sometimes singing and shouting, sometimes listening to a leader praying in short sentences, in words which they can understand and identify with.

   So if you avoid prayers in your group because you wonder what the relevance is to small children – and how are you going to get them quiet anyway? – try a different approach. Be creative with your own praying and let that creativity flow into your work with children.

   Each of the outlines includes a suggestion for 'creative prayer'. Like the other elements in the outlines, these can be used at any appropriate point in your programme, though sometimes you may need to do a particular activity first, eg making stars or ladybirds as a focus for prayer. Some suggestions encourage children to look, handle and respond to God; the end result of other 'creative prayer-times' will be something suitable for display as a reminder of the day's theme. We hope these suggestions will generate other ways of praying with young children – and that you will write and tell us about them. Some general guidelines are given below.

Activity prayers

- Draw a large tree – trunk and bare branches only – on a sheet of A3 paper. Have available cut-out shapes of leaves or fruit. Prayers are written on the leaves, which are then stuck on the tree. The youngest children could help to colour the trunk, and the leaves could have something as simple as one word on them, such as the name of someone they love and want to pray for. If they can manage, they could cut out the leaf-shapes themselves. Bringing the leaves to the tree and sticking them on is itself part of their praying.
- A variation on the prayer tree idea is to make hand prints with thick poster paint. These are cut out and stuck on the tree to make frondy leaves – particularly effective on a vine. Nothing would need to be written on these leaves: an overall caption like, 'Thank you, Jesus, that we belong to you,' and a one-sentence prayer by the leader along similar lines would be sufficient.
- Hand prints can also be used very effectively on a very large outline of a hand. A prayer here could be along the lines of, 'Thank you, God, that I am safe in your hands.'
- Alternatively, hand prints can be used in a session on Hands or Helping, with a caption like, 'Please, Jesus, help me to use my hands to be kind.'
- If it is impractical to use paint to make hand prints, the above ideas would be just as effective using outlines of the children's hands drawn on to green paper and cut out.

- Coloured strips of pre-gummed paper make lovely paper chains. A very effective prayer on themes around belonging in God's family is to let each child choose a strip of paper, and then help him to write his name on it. The strips are all linked together to make a chain. The children can hold the chain while they say a one-sentence prayer like, 'Thank you, God, that we all belong to your family', or sing a suitable song, eg 'God is our Father' or 'Jesus loves Kristi'.
- Almost any simple shape can be made into a prayer mobile – stars, fish, candles, faces etc – and the possibilities are limitless. A different word can be written on each of the shapes which are then strung up in a line, so that the whole makes a prayer. The children can draw their prayer on the shapes (eg someone they love) and assemble them to make a simple mobile which they take home. For instance, a circle with 'Jesus loves me' written on one side can be given to each child so that they can draw their own face on the other; the leader can then string up the faces and pray a one sentence prayer like, 'Thank you, Jesus, that you love us all.'
- Use a large piece of lining paper or sugar paper with a caption that fits the theme and let the children choose from a selection of suitable pictures. In turn, let them stick their picture on the paper, with them or the leader saying a short prayer. A seaside theme, for example, could have the caption, 'Thank you, God, for all the fun we have at the seaside,' and then the children could stick on anything that they especially enjoy – pictures of ice-creams, buckets and spades, waves, rocks, etc. As each child sticks on his picture, he or the leader might say, 'Thank you, God, for the waves/the sand/ice cream…'

Visual prayers

- In the past, children were taught to pray with their eyes shut in order to avoid being distracted. Using pictures also helps to focus their attention, and gives some visual input, too. So if the theme has been about creation, for example, try using a series of pictures that the children can look at as they are praying: 'Lord, you made ... Thank you.' Pictures may be postcards, line drawings, photos from calendars, or you could use OHP acetates or even a slide projector, depending on space and facilities.
- If you have a selection of pictures related to the theme, you could let each child choose one and encourage them to say a prayer based on the picture. A selection of pictures of different sorts of animals may stimulate prayers like, 'I like elephants' long trunks,' and so on. You can encourage the group to join in by saying 'Thank you, God' after each child's contribution. Remember, you are helping them to begin to express themselves to God, not looking for success or perfection. There will always be some children who won't want to join in, but it won't matter if you don't become anxious about it.
- A simple display (protected from curious fingers, of course!) can act as a focus. Try using flowers, a lighted candle, fruit or vegetables, even a birthday cake. If it is possible to sit the children in a circle around the display, so much the better. Remember how short a young child's concentration span is – three minutes at the most! Perhaps they could hold hands and sing a quiet song, or the leader could invite them to remember that Jesus is with them and that he loves them, maybe naming individual children: 'Jesus loves you, Ben, and you, Susie ...'

Quiet prayers

Occasionally it is entirely appropriate to spend a few moments in quiet, letting the presence of God himself touch the minds and spirits of the little ones in your care. 'Not easy with toddlers around!' we hear you cry, but if you want to try it, here are one or two suggestions.

- Many young children have a special 'cuddly' that they snuggle into when they are tired or wanting to be quiet – a blanket, a teddy, a pillow. Ask them to bring it with them one week and have some cushions available for them to rest their heads on.

  Play some quiet music – it need not necessarily be 'Christian', though it may be. Invite the children to sit or lie on the floor, snuggling up to their 'cuddly'. Some children may prefer to sit on Mum's knee to do this. Ask them to imagine the warmest, safest place they can think of – a place where they most like to be when they are tired or feeling quiet. It may be someone's knee, their own bed, the rug by the fire etc. (Don't assume that the safest place will be being cuddled by members of their family.)

  Remind them that Jesus is with them now, that he is always with them and that they are safe with him. Encourage them to stay quiet for a few moments listening to the music, and expect God's presence to touch them. It is an opportunity for the leaders to pray silently for the children, too. Then close with a one-sentence prayer like, 'Thank you, Jesus, for always being with us, whatever we are doing.'

  Keep it very short and be flexible; if you have planned something like this one week, but can't get the group quiet, don't worry. Have an alternative to fall back on and wait for another opportunity.
- If you have access to a fancy synthesiser you could try making a tape of soothing sounds using special effects – water falling, the seaside, bird calls etc. Depending on the sounds you use, and the theme, you could pray a one sentence prayer like; 'We love the sound of… Thank you, God, for creating it/ giving us ears to hear it/…'

Musical prayers

Songs can be used very effectively as prayers, either for enthusiastic worship, using instruments and actions, or for quieter, more reflective praying. Singing a quiet song is just as much 'prayer' as listening to a prayer being read, and often responded to better by little ones. Any of the songs suggested in the outline may be used, or your group's favourites.

Using set prayers

It is helpful to teach small children simple prayers, as much to help parents who are not comfortable praying with their children as for the children themselves. A mother may be able to say a simple prayer with her child at bed-time if it has been learned by rote, whereas she may feel embarrassed about talking to God spontaneously. Short prayers with a rhythm are the easiest for small children to remember.

Traditional prayers might include verses of hymns like 'Jesus, Friend of little children', or 'Jesus loves me, this I know', or short prayers drawn from the church's rich heritage, like 'God be in my head'.

Useful resource books include

Everyday Graces; *Everyday Prayers*; *Goodnight Prayers*; *Prayers for Special Days*; – all published separately by Lion in the series Little Lions Prayers, but also compiled into *My First Prayer Book*

(Treasure Press, ISBN 1 85051 320 1)

First Prayers – Original prayers, colourfully illustrated – by Helen Gompertz (Scripture Union, ISBN 0 86201 135 3)

First Prayers – Traditional prayers (Lutterworth Press, ISBN 0 7188 0306 X)

Let's Pray Together! – A book of prayers for the under-eights – by Geoffrey Marshall-Taylor (Collins, ISBN 0 00 599663 5)

The Lion Book of Children's Prayers – Traditional and original prayers for children, with photographs and line drawings – compiled by Mary Batchelor (Lion Publishing, ISBN 0 85648 070 3)

A Little Book of Prayers (Award Publications Ltd, ISBN 0 86163 385 7)

My Book of Prayers – Similar to *First Prayers* – by Helen Gompertz (Scripture Union, ISBN 0 85421 998 6)

■ HOW TO PLAN A PROGRAMME

The outlines in this book are presented in a form which makes them adaptable and easy to refer to, but not in a form which can be used directly in a specific situation – especially the more structured situation of a pram service. So how do you set about planning for a particular event?

- **First decide on your aim.** What do you want the children to know or have experienced at the end? As you can see from the outlines, this doesn't have to be anything complicated – that God loves them; that he made them; that Jesus wants them to be kind; to learn to say 'thank you'... Perhaps you simply want them to get to know a Bible story – a miracle Jesus did, a story he told, something about an Old Testament character... Of course, you might want them to *experience* something – praise and worship, for instance; the enjoyment of being together in church; a party...

   Keep in mind that young children tend to take things literally, so avoid abstract aims like, 'To teach the children that Jesus is the Light of the World.' That may be an appropriate focus for the adults, but for the children it would be best to stay with the fact that God gives us light to see by.

- **Having decided what you want the children to know, choose an appropriate theme.** For instance, if your aim is that the children learn something about prayer, you might decide on three separate themes over three sessions – 'Saying: Thank you, God'; 'Saying: Please God'; 'Saying: Sorry, God'.

- **The next thing to decide is which story best fits the theme. If there is a relevant Bible story, use it. But if one doesn't come to mind, find a good children's story to use instead.** Avoid using a Bible story out of context just because you feel you have to put one in. There will be enough Christian input in the rest of the session.

- **Next choose lots of songs to sing during the session.** Children love music, so if only one or two songs are consistent with the theme of the week, it doesn't matter if you sing them several times and sing lots of favourite songs as well. Include finger rhymes at this stage of your planning, too.

- **Now decide which activities you are going to include and plan the prayer time.**

- **Lastly, decide on your order**: where exactly are you going to put the story presentation... the creative prayer time...? When are you going to have the activities...? Which songs would be best

following the story...? When is it easiest to give out the instruments......?

However, whether you are planning for a toddler group with a five minute 'God slot' or a thirty minute pram service, you need to plan well in advance. We know from experience that once you are surrounded by twenty-five or thirty under-fives there is no time to think, let alone do any last-minute preparations!

An example will show how the planning process can change an outline into a detailed programme for a thirty minute pram service. Suppose that the outline is presented (as most are in this book) as:

- A Bible link with a focus for children and a focus for adults. The Bible passage could form the basis of a story. If the story is well-known or straightforward, we have left you to tell it as you wish. Sometimes we have suggested a brief story outline, or ways to dramatise it, or given main points to stress where Bible passages are less familiar or use stories normally considered too difficult or complicated for young children.

- A touch and talk idea. Touch and talk is intended to 'lead in' to the Bible story and form a link between the children's own experience and the world of the Bible.

- Activity ideas for craft work (collages and other things to make) and games. (Activities generally follow on or arise from the story. Where they can usefully precede the story we have put them with the introductory section.)

- A list of suitable songs and rhymes.

By the planning process outlined above this could be turned into the following service programme on the theme 'we all matter to God':

1. Three short, lively action songs. One of the songs – 'Thank you, Lord, for this fine day' – has nothing to do with the theme – which is we all matter to God – but that is not a problem. We sing it every week!
2. Touch and talk. Some almost complete jigsaws will prompt a hunt for the missing pieces and talk about how we lose things. Say that we'll have a story later about a woman who lost something.
3. A song which is especially relevant to the theme.
4. A feely-bag game. This, again, links with the theme: objects found in one bag have 'missing parts' lost in the other!
5. A story. The story of the lost coin (Luke 15) is told from the point of view of the woman whose coin was lost.
6. A finger rhyme which links with the theme.
7. Two or three lively songs accompanied with instruments like shakers, tambourines, drums and bells.
8. Some activities – including a creative prayer-time.
9. Hand out the Allabout sheets over refreshments.

SONGS AND RHYMES RESOURCE LIST

Rhymes written out in full are either traditional, new to this book, or have previously appeared in *Learning Together with Under-Fives* (Scripture Union). It is obviously imposible to print in full all the other finger rhymes, games and songs we recommend, so we have used several easily-available paperbacks. If you can only buy one or two books we recommend *Let's Join In* – specifically Bible geared – and *Five Furry Teddy Bears* – more general. Another good resource is *Junior Praise*. We also assume you have access to Ladybird books of traditional rhymes. Occasionally we give details of a song from another book. * indicates those with an action element. The following abbreviations are used:

Rhymes and songs

FFTB – *Five Furry Teddy Bears* – Contemporary action rhymes, finger plays, songs and games – by Linda Hammond (Puffin, 1990, ISBN 0 14 034151 X) Price £2.75

LJI – *Let's Join In* – A collection of biblically-based action songs and rhymes – compiled by Christine Wright (Scripture Union, 1990, ISBN 0 86201 622 3) Price £3.95

OTU – *Okki Tokki Unga* – Action songs for children – compiled by Beatrice Harrop, Linda Friend and David Gadsby (A & C Black, 1976, ISBN 0 7136 1685 7) Price £6.50

RRG – *Round and Round the Garden* – Play rhymes; first in a series of four, available also with audio cassettes at Early Learning Centres – by Sarah Williams (OUP, 1983, ISBN 0 19 272132 1) Price £2.50

TLP – *This Little Puffin* – Finger plays and nursery games – compiled by Elizabeth Matterson (Puffin, 1969, ISBN 0 14 030300 6) Price £2.99

Christian song books

CGC – *Carol Gaily Carol* – Carols and songs telling the Christmas story – compiled by Beatrice Harrop (A & C Black, 1973, ISBN 0 7136 1407 2) £4.95

CH – *Cry Hosanna!* – In the same series as SLW and FS also with some good children's songs not found anywhere else – compiled by Betty Pulkingham and Mimi Farra (Hodder and Stoughton, 1980, ISBN 0 340 25159 X)

CP2 – *Come and Praise 2* – compiled by Geoffrey Marshall-Taylor (BBC Publications, 1988, ISBN 0 563 34247 1)

CS – *Come and Sing* – Songs for the under-8's – compiled by Pamela Dowman and Elspeth M Stephenson (Scripture Union, 1971, ISBN 0 85421 301 5) Price £2.95

CSM – *Come and Sing Some More* – A sequel to *Come and Sing* – compiled by Ann Broad (Scripture Union, 1982, ISBN 0 85421 948 X) Price £2.95

IFW – *Ishmael's Family Worship* – A good resource of praise songs for all ages – by Ishmael (Kingsway Music, 1988, ISBN 0 86065 664 0) Price £4.99

JP – *Junior Praise* – Over 300 hymns and songs for children, including many old favourites – compiled by Peter Horrobin and Greg Leavers (Marshall Pickering, 1986, ISBN 0 551 01293 5)

MTB – *Merrily to Bethlehem* – Less well-known carols for the younger age-group – compiled by David Gadsby and Ivor Golby (A & C Black, 1978, ISBN 0 7136 1887 6)

SHF – *Songs and Hymns of Fellowship* (Kingsway, ISBN 0 86065 935 6) £19.99

SLW and **FS** – *Combined Sounds of Living Waters* and *Fresh Sounds* – An adult hymn book with some children's songs – compiled by Betty Pulkingham and Jeanne Harper (Hodder and Stoughton, ISBN 0 340 23262 5) Price £9.95

SSL – *Someone's Singing Lord* – Simple hymns and songs for the under-8's – compiled by Beatrice Harrop (A & C Black, 1984, ISBN 0 7136 1730 6) Price £6.50

At the end of the section on 'Music' is an additional list of songbooks and cassette tapes. These are further resources, not already mentioned in the outlines.

OUTLINE SERIES

make tape.

water trickling
Hoover
car
animals
(music
_____

St Francis.
How do we hear God?
How did God speak to
St Francis.

GOD MADE ME

Rhymes/songs suitable for every outline in the 'God made me' series:
* Heads, shoulders, knees and toes TLP 125
* My body LJI 22
* He gave me eyes SSL 19

■ EARS

■ **BIBLE LINK: Jesus heals a deaf man – Mark 7:31-37.**

■ **Focus for children:** to appreciate the sense of hearing and to realise that some people are deaf.

■ **Focus for adults:** Jesus took the man away from the crowd, and healed him privately. His care and sensitivity are just the same for each of us today.

Touch and talk

If you know someone with a pet rabbit, used to children, see if you can bring it in for them to look at its ears. Make sure that children (and adults!) who touch the rabbit wash their hands. Otherwise find soft toys with prominent ears – an elephant, for example, or a pig or a cat. Show the toys to the children pointing out the different kinds of ears. Ask the children to show you their ears; can they move their ears up and down, as animals like horses and dogs can? Can they flap their ears like elephants? What are ears for? At this point you could lead in to the listening activity below as part of your story presentation.

Listening activity

Pre-record a short tape, lasting about a minute, with familiar sounds, like a vacuum cleaner, a tap running, a phone ringing, a door closing, and perhaps the theme tune of a pre-schoolers' TV programme. Play it and ask the children what sounds they recognise. Alternatively you could record each of the above sounds with a short pause in between each, and stop the tape after each one, asking the children, 'What was that?' Point out that they know what it is because their ears picked up the sounds; if their ears didn't work, they wouldn't have been able to hear the tape. Use the word 'deaf' and explain that it means somebody who can't hear, and proceed with the Bible story.

■ ACTIVITIES
Creative prayer-time/visual display

Give each child a piece of paper and provide a selection of magazine pictures of things that make a noise – the choice is enormous. Write at the top of the paper 'X (child's name) likes to hear…' and let children choose what they like to hear – the washing-machine, aeroplanes, dogs barking, birds, the TV. This could be adapted for a visual display by drawing a large picture of an ear, and writing, 'These are the things we hear each day', and letting each child stick on a picture to represent an everyday sound – traffic, household noises, people, pets, radios, alarm clocks, etc. Use this time to thank God that we can hear and to pray simply for people who can't, perhaps using the words of the prayer below, while the children are sticking on their pictures.

> *Dear Lord Jesus,*
> *Thank you for ears to hear wonderful things in your world.*
> *Thank you that we can hear the birds and the animals.*
> *Thank you that we can listen to music and stories.*
> *Please help all the people who can't hear – especially deaf boys and girls.*
> *Amen.*

Making ears

Use sugar paper or thin card. Cut out, or let older children cut out, ear shapes. (If you have time and enough adult help, perhaps have a selection of animal ear shapes, and let the children choose which ears they'd like.) Let the children colour the ears, and then staple them to a band of paper about 5 cm wide, which should then be adjusted to fit the child's head and fastened with sticky tape. Let the children wear the ears for the rest of the session.

Making earrings

Cut circles of card about 5 cm in diameter, and punch a hole near the edge. Let the children decorate a pair with shiny paper, sequins, felt-tip pens, glitter etc. When they have finished, tie a piece of wool through the punched hole, long enough to loop over the child's ears. This may appeal more to girls, but let boys do it if they want to.

Guessing game

This is best played in small groups. Ask for a volunteer, and tell that child the name of an object or animal, eg phone or dog. They must then make an appropriate noise for the others to guess. The first correct guess makes the next noise. Have a list ready or you may go blank! Alternatively, you could have a number of pictures, from which you select at random, without looking, asking the group to make the noise so that you can guess which picture you've held up.

■ SONGS AND RHYMES

I'm very glad of God SSL 22
* Listen

Listen! listen! *(Cup hands to ears)*
What's that sound? *(Shake head from side to side)*
Where does it come from? *(Look puzzled)*
Look around: *(Look in all directions)*

Is it the traffic roaring by? *(Mime driving a car)*
Is it an aeroplane up in the sky? *(Shade eyes; look up)*
Is a cow saying, 'Moo moo moo'? *(Make ears - hands on head)*
Is an owl calling 'Tu whit tu whoo'? *(Circle eyes)*

My ears tell me such a lot! *(Point to ears)*
Thank you God for these ears I've got! *(Clap rhythmically)*

And see the list at the top of this page.

■ The Allabout sheet for this outline is on page 73.

■ MOUTH & TONGUE

■ **BIBLE LINK:** Joshua 6 – the battle of Jericho.

■ **Focus for children:** to discover what they can do with their mouths and to begin to learn that God has given them gifts of speech and taste.

■ **Focus for adults:** there are many places in the Psalms where we are exhorted to 'make a joyful noise to the Lord' (not necessarily musical!). Other places in scripture remind us that the words we say have great effect (James 3:1-12; Matthew 12:33-37). As we care for young children, it is worth bearing in mind that they absorb both words and intonation, and can be reassured or frightened by what they hear.

Touch and talk

Talk about how we use our mouths to make sounds, and which parts of our mouths we use.

• Ask the children to copy sounds like *la, la, baa, baa, mmm, mmm,* and so on. What sort of noise does the rain make; the wind; water going down the bath plug; a waterfall?

• Experiment to find out which kinds of sounds different parts of our mouths make: try making sounds with *closed* mouths... *open* mouths... just with the *lips*... with the *tongue*... with *teeth*... What happens to the sounds if they put their hands over their mouths...? Say *aahhh* and bang their chests...?

• Give each child the middle from a kitchen roll or toilet roll and ask them to try making different noises down it. Let the children have fun making lots of sounds.

• Explain to the children that we need all parts of our mouths to speak properly: people who can't speak at all are *dumb*.

• What else do we use our mouths and tongues for? Encourage the children to think about exactly how they use their mouths to eat and taste: which parts of their mouths do they need to eat an apple, for instance?

Story presentation

Explain that Joshua was a very brave friend of God, the leader of the Israelite army, and that God had told him to capture the city of Jericho in a very

unusual way.

Choose seven children to be the priests and give them each a kitchen-roll middle to be a trumpet.

Divide the rest of your group into the soldiers who went in front of the priests and the soldiers who went behind them. (It isn't necessary to include details about carrying the Ark.)

Show the children an imaginary 'Jericho' in the centre of the room. Tell them that it was completely surrounded by high walls and explain what the Israelites had to do.

March them six times round 'Jericho', with the priests blowing on their trumpets, to represent six days. Then march them round again and after the seventh time round tell the children that Joshua told everyone to use their voices. He didn't want them to whisper (whisper, 'God is with us!'). He didn't want them to talk (say 'God is with us!'). He wanted them to shout (shout 'God is with us!')!

When all the people shouted as loudly as they could (encourage all the children to shout), there was a shaking and a rumbling and banging and a quaking. The walls of the city wobbled and fell down. Then the people all shouted again, 'Hooray! God is with us!' and the soldiers marched in!

■ ACTIVITIES
Creative prayer-time

• The children repeat each line (except for the last, when they make their own 'praise' sounds), following the leader's voice.

Praise the Lord!
Praise him with a loud voice.
Praise him with a quiet voice.
Praise him with a singing voice.
Praise him with every sound
you can make!

Visual display – collage

Find pictures of objects that make different sounds, eg clock, cat, water.... Let the children choose a picture and then copy the sound. Make the pictures into a collage with a caption like, 'It's fun to make sounds; thank you, God.'

Rainbow book of mouths

Collect magazine pictures showing as many different expressions and as many different ways of using mouths as you can. You could even choose different kinds of animal mouths.... Have ready

some small books – one for each child – made out of different coloured pieces of paper. For each book you will need four or five pieces of A4 paper cut in half lengthways.

Stack the paper together so that the sheets overlap one another by about 1.5 cm. Fold near the centre so that the rainbow effect is continued all through the book. Punch two holes at the fold of the book and tie with ribbon, or staple it together along the folded edge.

Help the children to write on the front of the book, 'Thank you, God, that you make us all different', then let them choose pictures to stick into their books, one for each page. Encourage them to draw their own mouths on the last page and help them write, 'And I am special to you', underneath.

Sound games

• Try saying some tongue twisters. How about this one?

Skinny Winny, silly ninny,
took a bath.
Pulled the plug; glug, glug, glug.
That's the end of Skinny Winny!

• Bring a blank tape and let the children talk or sing into it. Many of them will not have heard their own voices before and will be fascinated by it. Try recording Mum, too. Does she sound right?

• Go on a bear hunt! (See page 30 for this activity)

Read a story

Sounds, sounds all around by Jean Watson (Little Lions Under Five's) is about hearing sounds, but could easily be adapted to this theme by encouraging the children to make the sounds in the book.

■ SONGS AND RHYMES

* God is our Father SF 132
* Thank you, Lord, for this fine day JP 232, CSM 6 – adapted to '... for mouths that talk ... tongues that taste ... lips to lick' etc.
* Let everyone clap hands with me OTU 2
* I will wave my hands in praise and adoration IFW 43
* Lord, you put a tongue in my mouth IFW 58
And see the list on page 23.

■ The Allabout sheet for this outline is on page 73.

■ NOSES

■ BIBLE LINK: Genesis 27:1-29 – Jacob's deception of Isaac.

■ Background: read Genesis 25 to see how the rivalry between Jacob and Esau began. According to the custom of the day, Isaac's blessing of Jacob was legally binding, and could not be reversed even though a mistake had been made.

■ Focus for children: to discover what their noses do, and to help them begin to learn that God has made them.

■ Focus for adults: in Genesis 25, the story is told of how Esau exchanged his birthright for a bowl of stew (verses 27-34). This story is its sequel. The blessing of the firstborn was held in higher esteem than the inheritance, and Esau is distraught when he realises that Jacob has stolen this from him too. Esau's fury results in Jacob's running away to live with his uncle. It is a salutary reminder of the importance of not showing favouritism within the family: the text shows how the boys' parents both had favourites.

Touch and talk

Have a selection of items to smell, eg a fragrant flower, a banana, cheese, leather, wool, toothpaste, soap, soil, etc. See if the children can identify them with their eyes closed.

Talk about favourite smells – and the smells they don't like! Explain that being able to smell means also being able to taste. Have they ever had a bad cold which has affected their taste? Perhaps one or two of the older children would be willing to try this experiment: ask them to hold their noses and try eating a piece of bread. Can they taste it?

Talk about how animals use their sense of smell and how important it is to them.

Story presentation

Introduce the story by talking about recognising people by their smell. Do the people they know well have a special smell? If space permits, you could see if the children can recognise their mothers by their special smell – young children are far more aware of smell than adults are, on the whole.

Then tell the story, either using OHP slides of appropriate pictures or using puppets or dressed-up dolls as visual aids. You could tell the story this way:

Isaac was very old and blind. He recognised the people around him by their voices and their smells. Best of all he liked the smell of his eldest son, Esau, when he had been out in the country, hunting.

Esau was out a lot. He used to catch wild goats and bring them for Isaac to eat. Isaac could always recognise Esau by his hairy arms and legs, and his outdoor smell.

Isaac enjoyed eating tasty meals. He especially liked eating the food that Esau caught and cooked for him. The smells from the cooking were delicious!

One day, Isaac asked Esau to hunt and prepare something really tasty, so that he could give him a special blessing and ask God to make him a very important person.

Jacob was Esau's twin brother. He wasn't at all like Esau – Isaac could always recognise Jacob by his smooth arms and legs, and his indoor smell – because Jacob spent most of his time indoors with his mother.

Now, though, Jacob was jealous of his brother. He wanted the special blessing instead of Esau. He decided to trick Isaac so that he'd be the one to get his father's blessing.

So, while Esau was out hunting, Jacob pretended to be Esau. He put hairy animal skins on his arms and dressed up in Esau's clothes so that he would feel just like Esau and smell just like Esau.

Then he took his father his favourite meal. Isaac asked, 'Who is it?'

Jacob said, 'I'm Esau, Father.'

Isaac shook his head. 'You sound like Jacob, but you feel like Esau and you smell like Esau – and this meal smells delicious!'

So he ate it all up and then he gave Jacob his special blessing instead of giving it to Esau.

When Esau found out what had happened, he was furious! He didn't think Jacob had been very nice. Do you?

■ ACTIVITIES
Creative prayer-time

• Collect pictures of faces with different sorts of noses – you could use people, animals, or birds. How about some clowns? Give each child a piece of coloured paper and let them choose several noses to stick on their piece of paper.

Write for them, or help them write: 'Noses God made.'

Then let the children stick their page of noses on to a large piece of paper to make a big collage. Write underneath, 'God made us all different. Thank you, God.'

Say together, with appropriate actions:

Red noses, white noses,
Pointed noses, stubby noses,
Long noses, short noses,
GOD made them all!

Funny noses

Collect kitchen-roll middles or fromage frais pots. Let the children paint or decorate them and then help them to cut them into a variety of funny nose shapes. Make a hole in each side and attach shirring elastic to keep them on.

A smelly poster!

Make a poster of different smells. Draw a large circle on a piece of strong paper and devide it into segments like a pie. Have as many segments as categories of smell: eg fragrant smells, food smells, unpleasant smells, dangerous smells, no smells. Find small objects and pictures for the children to stick on to each section. You could have some pieces of soap, a coffee bag, rose petals, etc. For dangerous smells use pictures or labels. Things with no smell might include pictures of water.

Make masks

Give each child a face-sized piece of card. Let them draw a face on and decorate it if they want to. Make holes for their nose and eyes.

Write on the mask: 'God has given me a … nose (big, little, snuffly, turned-up etc) and he loves me.'

■ SONGS AND RHYMES

* The butterfly song SLW 106; JP 94
* Put your finger on your head OTU 27
* Jump! – in the *Jump!* songbook from TMC Records, 960 Gateway, Burlington, Ontario, Canada L7L 5K7. Include a verse like 'Touch your nose'.

And see the list on page 23.

■ The Allabout sheet for this outline is on page 74.

■ FINGERS & SKIN

■ **BIBLE LINK: Naaman – 2 Kings 5:1-14.**
■ **Focus for children:** to appreciate the sense of feeling and touch and their skins.
■ **Focus for adults:** Naaman at first refused to follow Elisha's instruction because it was too easy. Jesus emphasised the importance of simple childlike trust. Sometimes God wants us to do something simple, and trust him to do the rest.

Touch and talk

Provide a variety of objects and substances for the children to feel, eg wet and dry sand, smooth and rough stones, soft and hard, spongy and rubbery, warm and cold. Talk about how they feel. How do we feel things? We feel with our fingers but also all over our bodies with our skin. We can feel a feather on our arms, or if we wear an itchy jumper; we feel uncomfortable if we have a stone or sand in our shoes. Often we know what things are without seeing them, just by the way they feel.

Story presentation

This story can be told using the outline below – which is 240 words long and takes just under two minutes to tell at a speed suitable for young children. Anything longer is too long at this stage. This story will be doubly effective if you use your body and mime dipping a toe in ('Ooh it's cold!'), dipping right under and seeing the result (open hands and arms wide, and look down at your body and smile), etc.

Have you ever had spots on your skin because you were ill? Did they itch? A man in the Bible once had very bad skin. His name was Naaman and he was a Very Important Soldier. But he had a dreadful skin disease and no one could make it better.

One day a little girl who worked in Naaman's house said, 'Why don't you go and see Elisha in my country? He's God's servant and he might make you better.'

Naaman set off with lots of presents, but when he got to Elisha's house, Elisha didn't even come out to see him! He just sent a message, 'Go and wash seven times in the river Jordan.'

Naaman was Very Cross! 'Huh!' he shouted, 'I'm not going to wash in that dirty old river, so there!' He started to go home in a temper but someone said to him, 'Why don't you just try it? It's not difficult.'

So Naaman went to the river. He put his toe in; he waded in up to his waist; he dipped right under the water – once – and came up. Nothing had happened. He went under again: that was twice.

Count with me: three…four… five…six… Still nothing happened!

Then he did it for the last time – number seven – and when he came out of the water his skin was ALL BETTER! Naaman said a big thank you to God!

Rhyme

1, 2, 3, 4, 5 and 6 times
Naaman washed in the river,
1, 2, 3, 4, 5 and 6 times,
he began to shiver!
1, 2, 3, 4, 5 and 6 times,
each time getting wetter;
1, 2, 3, 4, 5, 6, 7 times:
Naaman was better!

■ ACTIVITIES
Creative prayer-time

Use the items brought in for 'Touch and talk'; give one to each child and tell them to feel it as they stand in a circle and sing (to the tune 'Thank you for the world so sweet'):

Thank you, God, for giving us
Hands and skins and things to touch.
Rough and smooth, and hot and cold,
Furry things we like to hold.

or

Thank God, thank God, all you little children,
For our skin, for our skin,
Thank him, thank him, all you little children,
For the things we like to touch.

(To the tune 'Praise him, praise him'.)

Visual display – collage

Have ready face shapes in yellow, black or brown, and white or pink; let the children stick on hair made of wool – straight black wool for the Chinese, crinkly black for the Afro-Caribbean and brown or yellow for the European. (Crinkly wool can be obtained by using wool that has been knitted and unpicked.) Point out that whatever the colour of our skin, God loves us.

Action pictures

Prepare each child a piece of paper with a 'river' drawn on it and a slit cut in the 'river'. Prepare also some cut out figures of Naaman. Let the children colour the figure and the river (or stick on tissue paper to represent water. Then put Naaman in the slit, so that they can move him up and down in the river.

Feely-bags

Put into opaque paper bags (or shoe-boxes with a hole the size of a child's fist cut in the side) a number of objects that a child will be able to recognise by touch: a small toy car, a building brick, a spoon, a pine cone, a small teddy bear. Let the children take turns at guessing what is inside and whispering the answer to an adult.

Fingerprinting

Use black paint for fingerprinting; if you mix the powder with washing up liquid or hand cream it will wash off much more easily. Point out that everyone has a different pattern on their fingers. Or use bright paints for handprints.

Finger puppets

Make simple finger puppets from two pieces of felt in an elongated thimble shape. If no felt is available, make puppets from strips of paper on which you can draw faces before you fasten them round their fingers with sticky tape.

Playdough

Even if you don't normally provide this, it would be good to have it as an activity today. Much of the fun for children is in feeling and moulding it, so it's a good illustration of the fact that God gives us fingers and skin to feel and touch. For recipe see page 13.

■ SONGS AND RHYMES

Use as many finger-rhymes as possible: ones children already know such as 'Incey wincey spider' or 'Round and round the garden' or find new ones in a book such as the *Ladybird Book of Finger-Rhymes*.

■ The Allabout sheet for this outline is on page 74.

■ HANDS & ARMS, LEGS & FEET

■ **BIBLE LINK: the healing of the lame man at the Beautiful Gate of the temple – Acts 3:1-11.**
■ **Focus for children**: to appreciate all they can do with their limbs.
■ **Focus for adults:** the lame man asked for money, but was healed in Jesus' name; sometimes God, in his great love, gives us something different from what we ask, because he knows what is best for us.

Touch and talk

Find a space and spend some time doing very simple exercises using arms and legs – stretching up and out to the side with arms, shaking arms from shoulders and wrists, bending elbows, touching toes, standing on tiptoe, bending knees, jogging on the spot, perhaps some hopping, though younger children often lack the co-ordination to do this, and leg-shaking. If possible play a tape of lively music while you exercise. At the end say something like, 'Didn't we do a lot of different things with our arms and legs? Wasn't it fun? God made our arms and legs didn't he?'

Story presentation

Introduce the story by saying that we are glad to be able to do so many things with our arms and legs, but some people's arms and legs don't work. Such people can often do things which able bodied people can't – like mouth or foot painting, wheel chair sports and even wheel chair dancing!

■ ACTIVITIES
Creative prayer-time/visual display

Warning: this is a messy activity! Protect the floor with newspaper or old sheets, and have plenty of warm water, soap and towels ready! Enlist plenty of adult help and give yourselves time. Footprints can be done only one at a time, so it might be a good idea to run another activity simultaneously so that children don't get bored and restless whilst awaiting their turn.

Help each child to put one (or both) bare foot/feet in a shallow tray of brightly coloured, fairly thick, water-based paint. Then the child steps on to a large piece of strong paper – on a pad of newspaper – onto which you have already put his/her initials. Wash and dry feet thoroughly. (This popular activity can also be done with hands, but this is a suggested activity for other topics.) If your premises or time don't allow you to make prints with paint, you can draw round feet or hands and let the children colour them in, or use coloured paper for the hand and foot shapes and mount them on a contrasting sheet. As each child's hand or foot is drawn, write his/her name on it and say, 'Thank you God for Katy's feet, and all the things she can do with them,' or when all the footprints are finished let children hold up their own, and all shout together, 'Thank you, God, for feet!'

Sock puppets

You will need an old sock for each child (or ask in advance for everyone to bring one), some circular sticky labels in bright colours, some felt and fabric glue (optional) and scissors. Put the sock over the child's arm so that his/her hand is in the foot. Stick on two labels (chosen by child) for eyes, and add a tongue cut from felt. Show the child how to move the puppet. (You could add ears or a hat or scarf…)

Gluing

Let the children cut out and/or stick pictures of shoes onto paper. (This apparently pointless occupation is much enjoyed by most children who learn valuable hand–eye co-ordination skills in the process.)

Matching activity

This takes more preparation but if you have a small group, or an artist and access to a photocopier, it could be worth doing. Prepare for each child a sheet of paper; on the right hand side stick or draw three or four different people – a footballer or jogger, a baby or small child, a smartly dressed lady, and say a child in wet-weather gear – but cut off their feet. On the left hand side of the paper, in a different order, stick the appropriate footwear. Get the children to match the shoes with the wearers. As the children do this activity, you can talk to them about feet, the different things we can do with them and the way they grow.

■ SONGS AND RHYMES

* Stand up, clap hands SSL 14
Hands to work SSL 21
Jesus' hands were kind hands SSL 33
* My hands and feet LJI 23
Jesus is your friend LJI 108
* Here we go round the mulberry bush – traditional. Choose things that involve arms and legs, hands and feet – brush our teeth/hair, run upstairs, kick a ball, point our toes, bend our knees, wiggle our fingers, stroke our pets…
* TLP has two sections of songs and action rhymes for hands and feet, beginning on pages 117 and 137 respectively.
* Follow me FFTB 160
* Training FFTB 152
* Boots and shoes FFTB 154
* Hokey cokey (traditional)
* My hands RRG 27
* Clap, clap hands RRG 10
And see the list on page 23.

■ The Allabout sheet for this outline is on page 75.

■ EYES

■ **BIBLE LINK: Jesus heals a blind man – Mark 10:46-52.**
■ **Focus for children:** to appreciate the sense of sight, especially the ability to see colours, and to understand that some people are blind or visually impaired.
■ **Focus for adults:** the blind beggar refused to be 'shut up' by the crowd; Jesus rewarded his faith and persistence.

Touch and talk

• Look at and handle a number of items connected with seeing: a pair of old spectacles, several cheap magnifying glasses, perhaps a kaleidoscope and a pair of binoculars, though under-fives generally find it difficult to close just one eye, so can't really appreciate the wonders of a kaleidoscope.
• If you could find some sheets of coloured cellophane or plastic for them to look through, that too is a fascinating activity – the world looks very interesting when it's all red!
• Encourage the children to talk, especially about eyes and eye-colours – let them see how many different colours there are in people's eyes.
• Alternatively, have a large bunch of colourful flowers or a bowl of fruit or bright vegetables for the children to look at; point out that if they couldn't see they wouldn't understand about colours.

Story presentation

Introduce this story with perhaps a picture of someone with a guide-dog, and explain that in Jesus' time people didn't have such things as guide-dogs or spectacles. Don't assume that children understand the word 'blind'.

■ ACTIVITIES
Creative prayer time/visual display

In the centre of a large sheet of paper, stick a colourful picture of something lovely to look at – perhaps flowers or a display of fruits, a beautiful landscape or baby animals. Let the children choose pictures of eyes cut from magazines and stick them all round the edge; label the poster 'Thank you, God, for eyes to see all the lovely things you have made.'

Sing 'He gave me eyes' (SSL 19) or 'I'm very glad of God' (SSL 22).

Eye picture

Draw simple face-shapes, one for each child, with two large ovals for eyes; let them colour the eyes to match their own. Write underneath: 'My name is… and my eyes are… God loves me.'

Making things

• **Binoculars:** talk briefly about what people use binoculars for, eg birdwatching and plane-spotting. Let children decorate and then glue together two toilet-roll middles, or similar tubes, to make pretend binoculars.
• **Spectacles:** help the children make specs out of pipe-cleaners; this is a very simple activity but for some reason children love to do it. While making the spectacles, talk about why people wear glasses; if a child in the group wears them, make them feel very special and important!

■ SONGS AND RHYMES

* I'm very glad of God SSL 22
* When Goldilocks went to the house of the bears OTU 18
* Here are Grandma's spectacles RRG 23, TLP 35 (variant)
And see the list on page 23.

■ The Allabout sheet for this outline is on page 75.

Songs suitable for every outline in the 'Creation' series:
    Who put the colours in the rainbow? JP 288
    Thank you for the world you made LJI 13
    All things bright and beautiful – selected verses and chorus
    God made the grass LJI 12

■ BIRDS & THINGS THAT FLY

■ **BIBLE LINK: Genesis 1:20-23 – God made the birds and all flying things.**
■ **Focus for children:** God made all winged creatures and cares about them.
■ **Focus for adults:** Jesus talked about birds (Matthew 6:26-30) to demonstrate our value to God and to remind us that as God provides for them he will provide for us too if we trust him.

Touch and talk

If possible bring in a bird in a cage – preferably one from a home with children. Secure the cage door firmly! Let the children look at and talk about the bird. Point out wings, feathers and beak. What does it like to eat? Does it need a drink? How many toes has it got? What noise does it make? If you meet in a room where children can see out of the windows, let them see if they can spot any more birds. Ask what other creatures have wings and perhaps show pictures of ladybirds, bees and butterflies etc. A picture of a bat would also interest small children. Ask who made these creatures.

Story presentation

In talking to the children about flying creatures and showing pictures etc you have probably covered most of what you would say in a 'story', so just reinforce the fact that God made all flying creatures – and was pleased with what he had made. Use one of the songs below – perhaps teach the children at this point 'Beetles and ants and butterflies too'.

■ ACTIVITIES
Creative prayer-time

If you have made any flying creatures – see below – let the children hold them and say the rhyme 'Things with wings' as a thank you to God. Otherwise, leaders could hold pictures of some of the creatures mentioned as a visual focus. The rhyme is short enough for small children to learn quickly and they would enjoy saying it more than once.

> *Thank you, God,*
> *for things with wings,*
> *That fly up high into the sky.*
>
> *Butterflies and moths and bees,*
> *Ants and bats and birds in trees,*
> *Thank you, God, for these.*

Bird poster

Provide a large (1 m by 60 cm) outline of parrot or other exotic bird. Help children draw round their hands and colour the outlines with crayons, paints or felt tips. Stick all the hands on the bird outline with fingers pointing down – to give a feather effect.

Butterflies

Cut simple butterfly shapes out of strong paper. Make them symmetrical with a fold down the middle. Let children paint a design in bold colours and thick paint on one half of the shape. Fold down the mid-line, press gently and unfold carefully – the design will be 'printed' on the other half as well.

Ladybirds

Cut oval shapes from red paper, or let children colour ovals red. Put a black line down the middle. Have ready six legs and several black spots for each child to glue on. They may need tactful guidance to get three legs each side! A head can be put on one end with a black felt-tip pen.

Bees

This could be a group or an individual activity. Prepare one large or several small bee shapes in stiff paper. Mark divisions for stripes, and let children stick on scraps of fabric or scrunched-up tissue paper in yellow/orange and dark colours. Possibly complete with white tissue paper wings (or a piece of net curtain for a large collage) and perhaps pipe-cleaner antennae. You could make a striking display by mounting all the bees on a blue background with flowers cut from wrapping paper or made by the children on another occasion.

Birds

Let children cut and/or stick pictures of birds from old cards onto paper. This is a good hand–eye co-ordination exercise.

■ SONGS AND RHYMES

* Beetles and ants and butterflies too:

There are beetles and ants and
    butterflies too,
*(Walk fingers; link thumbs and move
    hands for butterfly wings)*
Ladybirds, flies and bees (buzz buzz).
There are bats and moths that fly at
    night,
(Flap hands and arms for wings)
And birds that sing in the trees (tweet
    tweet).
(Make tree shape with hands)

To all of these creatures God gave
    wings.
(Point upwards for God)
He didn't give wings to me! No! No!
(Shake head vigorously)
But I watch and I listen as they go by
*(Point to eyes and ears and move
    head as if watching)*
And thank God for eyes to see!

* Insect party FFTB 136
* Let's crawl FFTB 139
* Pollen hunt FFTB 144
* A big busy bee FFTB 147
* Monty moth FFTB 148
* The bird is on her nest FFTB 20
* How many birds? FFTB 134
* Two little dicky birds (traditional)
* Here is the beehive RRG 34
* This little bird RRG 47
Ladybird, ladybird (traditional)
And see the list on this page.

■ The Allabout sheet for this outline is on page 76.

■ WILD ANIMALS

■ **BIBLE LINK: Psalm 104** – note that this is not intended to be 'the story' this week, rather a focal point for leaders to reflect on and perhaps share with adults in the group.

■ **Focus for children:** God made all wild animals in their wonderful diversity. He wants us to enjoy them and care for them.

■ **Focus for adults:** God created the earth and all the creatures in it. He cares for his creation, providing food for the wild creatures, as this psalm shows. Conservation is important.

Touch and talk

Provide a selection of pictures of wild and zoo animals. If you can find small models of animals as well, which the children can handle and talk about, so much the better. You can often buy these quite cheaply in packets in newsagents and toyshops. Another possibility is soft toys which come in all varieties and which children would enjoy handling. Get the children to name as many as possible, and point out that real animals are much bigger. (One of my children was speechless at the size of the hippos the first time she went to the zoo; it simply hadn't occurred to me that, having only seen pictures, and being used to domestic pets, she probably expected a hippo to be the size of a rabbit!) Point out obvious characteristics – the elephant's trunk, the camel's hump, the rhino's horn, and ask the children if they've been to a zoo or safari park, and what they saw there. Ask if they know who made all these animals.

Story presentation

This week, use a picture book about a zoo or a safari park, or a children's story. Tell or read it to the children, showing the pictures as you do. At the end, ask them who made all the animals, and remind them, if you don't get the answer, that God did. Some possible stories are: *Topsy and Tim go to the Zoo* by Jean and Gareth Anderson (Blackie, ISBN 0 216 92464 2); *Dear Zoo* by Rod Campbell (Puffin, ISBN 0 14 050446 X); *Zoo Walk* (unusual but striking black and white pictures) by Greg Reyes (OUP, ISBN 0 19 279795 6); *Postman Pat's Safari* by John Cunliffe (Andre Deutsch). If none of these appeals or is available, all children's libraries have a good selection of books suitable for pre-schoolers about zoos. Encourage children to talk about their own experiences of the zoo. If circumstances permit, and you can find a short video or extract from a longer wildlife documentary, you could show the children this instead of telling a story. Remember to reinforce the fact that God made all the animals you've seen – and the ones you haven't!

■ ACTIVITIES
Creative prayer time/visual display

Have a long backing sheet in white, brown, or light green and make a jungle frieze. Let children cut round wild animal silhouettes, or colour them in, and add some palm trees – the children could do these too if you have time, perhaps adding leaves cut from crepe paper. Glue (or staple if you have a staple gun) these silhouettes to the background and thank God for all the different animals.

If you know the songs 'If I were a butterfly' or 'Who's the king of the jungle?' they would be appropriate to sing – with actions – as the animals are being attached to the frieze.

Bear hunt

The leader says each line and children repeat it, with appropriate tones of voice, facial expression and actions; this rapidly turns into a chant.

Refrain (accompanied by rhythmic thigh-slapping)
We're going on a bear hunt.
We're going to catch a big one.
I'm not scared!
What a beautiful day! *(Look around in appreciation)*
Oh – oh... *(Apprehensive tone)*

Grass – long wavy grass.
Can't go under it,
Can't go over it,
Can't go round it,
We'll have to go through it.
Swish, swish, swish. *(Push way through imaginary grass)*

Refrain

Mud – thick, squelchy mud.
Can't go... etc
(Make squelching, slurping noises with mouths and pull feet out of thick mud)

Refrain

A river – a whirly swirly river.
(Swimming action and splash, splash, splash)

Refrain

A forest – a thick tall forest.
(Stumble trip, stumble trip and mime pushing through undergrowth)

Refrain

A cave – a deep dark cave. *(Say this slowly)*
(No actions for this one – continue as follows:)
Two big staring eyes. *(Point to eyes)*
One cold wet nose. *(Point to nose)*
Four big furry paws – *(Hold hands forward)*
IT'S A BEAR! *(Hands back in horror)*
Quick! – Home!
(As fast as possible with appropriate actions)
Out of the cave, through the forest, stumble trip, stumble trip, across the river, splash, splash, splash, through the mud, squelch, squelch, squelch, through the grass, swish, swish, swish – phew! We're home!

Animal montages or collages

Prepare some large outlines of easily recognisable animals – such as elephant, hippo, giraffe, – and coloured thin paper (eg magazine pictures of approximately the right colours) for the children to tear up and stick on to the outline.

Elephant trunks

Use a dark (preferably grey but it doesn't really matter) old sock – a man's or a child's long one, or even the leg of an old pair of ladies' tights. Stuff with newspaper, and attach firmly to a band of grey sugar paper which goes round the child's forehead – like a sweatband. The 'trunk' hangs down in front, and – hey presto! – an elephant.

Animal masks

Animal masks – like the lion illustrated here or the sheep mask on page 43 – can be made from paper plates. Use wool for hair and pipe cleaners for whiskers. Shirring elastic will hold the mask on.

Crocodiles

Draw or trace a simple crocodile shape like the one illustrated, omitting the upper jaw, and cut out one for each child. Draw the upper jaw separately and attach with a brass-headed paper fastener so that the mouth will open and close! Let children colour their crocodiles.

■ SONGS AND RHYMES

TLP has a selection of rhymes and games about zoo animals beginning on p 99.
* Who's the king of the jungle? JP 289
Have you seen the pussy-cat sitting on the wall? JP 72
* If I were a butterfly JP 94
* I went to the animal fair OTU 11
From the tiny ant to the elephant CP2
* Hedgehog wakes up FFTB 18
* Polar bear FFTB 36
* Put your finger in foxy's hole TLP 89
And see the list on page 29.

■ The Allabout sheet for this outline is on page 76.

■ FLOWERS & PLANTS

■ **BIBLE LINK: Genesis 2:8-10 – God's garden, the garden of Eden.**
■ **Focus for children:** God has made an amazing variety of plants and flowers for us to enjoy – by looking at them and smelling them.
■ **Focus for adults:** God delights in variety and abundance, colour and fragrance; he wants us to enjoy his gifts.

Touch and talk

Let the children look at seed catalogues, or publicity material for local gardens open to the public (obtainable from a tourist information office), or a couple of robust potted plants, and handle watering cans, packets of seeds, flower pots, seed trays, even small trowels and forks. Ask what you would use them for, and talk about gardens – who's got one, who's been to a local park (which is like a big garden), does anyone have plants indoors at home, or in a window box on a window-sill? Do they know that once God made a very special garden?

Story presentation

Have ready prepared a background – say half blue for sky, half green for the earth/grass, and a number of small pictures drawn or cut from magazines – trees, flowers, shrubs etc, with little blobs of Blu-tack on the back. Tell the story of God making a beautiful garden, asking the children to suggest what might have been in it. Try to incorporate all suggestions – flowers (pretty and smelling lovely), trees to give shade from the sun, trees with fruit or nuts for food, plants to feed the animals in the garden, everything anyone could want – the best garden ever! And God made it all. We plant seeds and bulbs, even trees, but God makes them grow.

■ ACTIVITIES
Creative prayer-time

(Adapt this miniature gardens idea according to the size and capabilities of your group: if you have just four or five children of two and a half upwards, try a communal garden in a fairly deep seed tray. If you have more than five, enlist some adult help and make individual gardens.) Choose fairly deep containers – about 5 cm if possible, eg used tin foil dishes. Fill the containers with soil or a mixture of sand and soil, well dampened, so that things stay put. Have ready a selection of leafy twigs, small flowers, and anything else children might like to put in a garden – small stones, or gravel, milk bottle tops or pieces of foil (to make water), etc. Avoid berries or beads, which children might put up their noses or in their mouths or ears! Have as much as you can as children prefer quantity to quality in an activity of this kind. Let them make gardens, with adults giving discreet help if needed. Talk about the fact that we are making gardens just as God made the very first garden. When all are finished, let the children hold their gardens, if they have made individual ones, or stand round the communal one, while you sing an appropriate thank you song such as this (to the tune: 'Thank you, Lord, for this fine day'):

Thank you, Lord,
for flowers and plants, (x 3)
In our gardens.

Flowers 1

Cut up coloured polystyrene egg-box bottoms, or paint or decorate plain cardboard ones, to use as flower heads. Make a hole with a pencil point in the back of each 'flower' and insert a 'bendy' straw (available in most supermarkets and large stationers). Bend the top of the straw over so that the flower head is at right angles to the straw. Children could make several of these and put them in a decorated yoghurt pot, anchored with Plasticine or a blob of plaster of Paris or Polyfilla, or they could make a posy by wrapping a lacy paper doily around them.

Flowers 2

Cut circles of coloured tissue paper about 8 cm in diameter, and let children choose about six. Position these on top of one another, and let an adult staple the centre to a piece of paper. Show the children how to gently squash the topmost two circles to make a flower centre and then 'pinch and push' the lower four to give realistic flower petals. Let children draw in stems and leaves.

Gardens

Give each child a piece of paper, plain or divided into blue sky and green/brown earth. Let them cut out and/or stick on pictures cut from seed catalogues or advertisements.

Planting seeds

Plant cress (see 'Fruit and vegetables' page 37) or give each child a flowerpot, egg box or yoghurt pot with a drainage hole in the bottom. Have ready soil or potting compost or a mixture of both, and let the children fill their containers – they'll make a mess but will love it! Make sure nobody eats it, and moisten the mixture before planting a few flower seeds to take home. (Something like candytuft, pansies, marigolds or nasturtiums would be suitable.) Remind them to water the seeds regularly, and tell parents the seedlings may have to be transplanted to a bigger pot later. An alternative would be to plant seeds earlier at home and bring seedlings ready for transplanting. This means children have more to watch as they don't have to wait for the seeds to germinate, but seedlings are easily damaged if handled too enthusiastically by pre-schoolers.

■ SONGS AND RHYMES
* Growing FFTB 16
* Oh what shall we do in our garden? TLP 41
* Flowers grow like this TLP 43
* We are going to plant a bean TLP 48
See also the list on page 29.

■ The Allabout sheet for this outline is on page 77.

GOD MADE TREES & WOOD

■ **BIBLE LINK: Luke 19:1-8 –** **Zaccheus climbs a tree.**

■ **Background:** tax-collectors were hated by fellow Jews because they worked for the occupying Roman forces. They were not paid a wage so extracted as much as they could from those liable to tax – hence their unpopularity.

■ **Focus for children:** God made trees and wood to be beautiful and useful for many things.

■ **Focus for adults:** God accepts us as we are, just as Jesus accepted Zaccheus, despised by others. An alternative focus is Psalm 1:3 – those who trust God are like trees planted near water; they don't 'dry up'.

Touch and talk

Bring in things made of wood – ornaments, salad bowl, bread board, building blocks, wooden toys or jigsaws; you could also provide a selection of twigs, conkers, acorns, and pine cones as well as leaves from a tree and a log. Encourage the children to talk about and handle the items; do they know what they have in common? What else in the room is made of wood? We can make things out of wood, but we can't make trees! Only one person can do that – God. God makes trees – all kinds of trees.

Story presentation

Ask if any children have ever climbed a tree; then say that a man in the Bible once climbed a tree to see Jesus, and proceed with the story.

■ ACTIVITIES
Creative prayer-time

Stand in a circle and give each child something tree-related to hold. Remind them that the things they are holding came from a tree – and God made it. Sing (tune: 'Thank you for the food we eat')

Thank you God for making trees,
Acorns, conkers, pine cones,
leaves.
Thank you too for wooden toys –
Lots of fun for girls and boys!

Visual display

Make a large tree outline, to which children can add leaves (simple shapes drawn on sugar paper for older children to cut out, or pre-cut shapes for children to paint or colour) and/or pictures of small animals and birds cut from old greetings cards.

Tree models

Use cardboard tubes (suitably anchored) for tree trunks, and scrunched-up tissue, newspaper or green crepe paper for foliage.

Bark-rubbings

Use medium-sized pieces of dry bark; help children hold a piece of paper over the bark and rub gently with a pencil or wax crayon.

Autumn trees/spring trees

Have ready tree trunks in brown paper and let the children add leaves of paper in autumn colours – red, orange, yellow, gold, brown, or get a slightly different effect with scrunched up tissue paper. In spring, do the same thing, but let the children stick on leaves of bright green and 'blossom' of pink and white tissues.

Sawdust and wood shavings

If you can get hold of these, they can be very interesting for children. You could simply let children play with them – learning about textures is an important part of their development. Wood-shavings fascinate them, and can be used in collage, eg as hair, but avoid shavings from very resinous wood as these can cause problems for children with sensitive skin or eczema. Sawdust has some of the properties of sand – it can be poured, moulded when damp and even coloured with paint or food-dyes, but it needs to be checked for splinters and handled with care as it can blow into eyes.

■ SONGS AND RHYMES

Who's that sitting in the sycamore tree? SSL 32
TLP 89-96 – a complete section of rhymes to do with trees
Signs of autumn FFTB 31
* Falling fir trees FFTB 125
* The beech tree FFTB 126
* The autumn leaves have fallen down TLP 61
* The cherry tree RRG 46
* The apple tree RRG 6
See also the list on page 29.

■ The Allabout sheet for this outline is on page 77.

GOD GIVES US ■ BREAD

■ **BIBLE LINK: the boy with the loaves and fishes – John 6:1-13.**
■ **Focus for children:** God gives us a very basic food – bread.
■ **Focus for adults:** just as Jesus accepted the boy's gift and used it to help many, so he will accept what we bring to him, however insignificant it may seem to us.

Touch and talk
Bring samples of different kinds of bread – white and brown, pitta bread, muffins etc. If possible have bread dough for the children to poke and prod, and some grains of wheat for them to feel as well. Encourage conversation about which bread they like and what they spread on it.

Story presentation
A simple visual aid such as a small basket covered with a tea towel, containing bread rolls and fish – perhaps cut out of paper – would add to the story.

■ ACTIVITIES
Creative prayer-time/visual display
Children could cut pictures of bread from magazines, or colour and paint loaf and roll shapes to make a 'bread collage' or a baker's shop, or even a banner/poster saying 'Give us each day our daily bread'. Sing:

Prayer

> ***Thank you for the food we eat,***
> ***Bread and butter, milk and meat.***
> ***Fruit and fish the boats bring in,***
> ***Thank you, God, for everything.***

Cooking
Make bread! See page 14 for how to do this with a group of under-fives.

Modelling
Use clay or modelling dough to make 'rolls' and 'loaves' of different shapes, eg twisted together to make a plait, small on large round to make a cottage loaf.

Bible story picture
For each child cut a round shape in a neutral colour for a picnic basket, five bread roll shapes and two fish shapes.

Let the children stick the 'loaves and fishes' in the basket.

■ SONGS AND RHYMES
Enough for all LJI 70
Two fish and five little loaves LJI 73 (probably the most suitable for under-fives)
Jesus feeds the crowd LJI 72
Pat a cake, pat a cake, baker's man (traditional)
* Finger rhyme, Five bread rolls in a baker's shop (this is an adaption of a traditional counting song, in which at first all five digits of one hand are held up and one is lowered each time the girl buys a roll):

Five bread rolls in a baker's shop,
Golden brown and shiny on the top.
Along came a girl with some money one day,
Bought a bread roll and took it right away.

Four bread rolls in a baker's shop, etc.

* Rhyme for movement: 'The farmer sows the seed' (tune: 'The farmer's in his den').

The farmer sows the seed,
The farmer sows the seed,
E I E I
The farmer sows the seed.
(Mime sowing seed by hand)

God sends the rain and sun, *(etc)*
(Mime rain with fingers and show sun by circling arms)

The wheat grows tall and straight, *(etc)*
(Mime wheat growing with hands and arms travelling upwards)

The farmer cuts it down, *(etc)*
(Mime action of scythe)

The miller grinds the flour, *(etc)*
(Mime grinding: upper palm in circular motion over lower)

The baker makes the bread, *(etc)*
(Mime kneading dough)

We all eat the bread, *(twice)*
Yum yum, yum yum, *(rub tummies)*
We all eat the bread.

Thank you God for bread, *(etc)*

(Display words if you want parents to join in; they're much more self-conscious than pre-schoolers!)

■ The Allabout sheet for this outline is on page 78.

Title in bold please

12 copies in all

34

■ WATER

■ **BIBLE LINK: John 4:3-30, 39-42 – the woman at the well.**

■ **Background:** the woman was astonished that Jesus not only spoke to her, but asked a favour. Jews and Samaritans were long-standing enemies; Samaritans were descendants of Israelites who had intermarried with other races and were despised for this by the Jews. The Samaritans built their own temple nearby and it is to this that the woman refers in verse 20.

■ **Focus for children:** God made water and provides it for us.

■ **Focus for adults:** Jesus offered the woman at the well 'living water' – the satisfaction of her deep spiritual thirst. Five times divorced, she was a reject of Samaritan society – the disciples were quietly horrified to find Jesus talking to her (verse 27) – yet Jesus accepted her totally and offered her new life; he does the same for us.

Touch and talk

Bring in a selection of 'clues' – toothpaste and a toothbrush, soap/shampoo and towel, face flannel, inflatable armbands, kettle, washing-up liquid, detergent for clothes. Say something like ' I'm going to be **very** busy today – I'm going to wash my face, clean my teeth, wash my hair, have a cup of tea, and wash up the cup and saucer, then do my washing, and then I think I'll go for a swim....' As you mention each activity, pick up the appropriate equipment. Then ask – have I got everything I need? Hopefully someone will remark that you need water for all the things you've talked about. Discuss with the children what they have used water for already today, and what other things they will do with it when they get home. Everyone needs water – lots of it. We get ours from taps, but some people get it from wells; in Bible times people got water from wells, and there's a story about Jesus at a well.

water the plants!

Story presentation

You will need to abbreviate the story because the conversation between Jesus and the woman is far too complicated for under-fives. The 'bare bones' of an appropriate story are... It was a hot day, and Jesus, on a journey, was tired and

thirsty. His friends had gone to get some food as it was lunch-time and Jesus sat down on the side of the well to rest (if possible show a simple picture of a well). The people in the village weren't very friendly, and a lady whom nobody liked came to fill up her water pot (show picture). Usually people didn't come to get water from the well in the middle of the day because it was much too hot. This lady came then because nobody spoke to her if she went with the others to the well early in the morning. Jesus asked her for a drink of water; she was very surprised that he even spoke to her. They talked for a long time, and the lady realised that Jesus was a very special person – God's Son.

■ ACTIVITIES
Creative prayer-time

Head a poster, 'We need water – God gives us water', and let the children stick on pictures cut from catalogues of, for example, baths/bathrooms, kettles, swimsuits or swimming pools, washing machines and kitchens, even garden hoses and watering cans. As each child sticks on his/her picture thank God for water for…washing, swimming, watering the garden etc…

Water play

Children love water and are fascinated by it. If you can possibly arrange it, try to provide water play for this week. If this is not a regular feature of your group, warn adults in advance to bring overalls or dry clothes for children! You don't need anything elaborate – newspapers and a sheet of polythene on the floor, an old baby bath with warm water, and plastic jugs, mugs, funnels and bottles (old shampoo bottles etc). If you wish you could add food colouring to the water or use a very mild baby shampoo to make it bubbly.

Water picture

Give each child a circle or strip of blue paper and let them stick on cut out shapes of water creatures – fish, tadpoles, frogs (see 'Rain', page 56) etc. Or let them add more exotic creatures like hippos and crocodiles!

Fire and water

• Remind children that water puts out many fires. Talk about fire engines and fire-fighters and read one of the

'Fireman Sam' stories.

• If you give them enough notice, local firemen might be prepared to come and talk about fire-safety, though the emphasis would then be more on fire than water, and the men might not be used to talking to pre-school children. Alternatively, you could use this outline to coincide with a local fire station's Open Day – generally a very exciting affair.

■ SONGS AND RHYMES

Fred Bumble FFTB 70
Bath-time FFTB 72
* Dirty teeth FFTB 156
Ivor the diver FFTB 108
* Doing the washing FFTB 64
London's burning (traditional)
TLP has a section 'Things we see near water' 109–116
* Here we go round the mulberry bush – traditional, but choose activities requiring water, like those mentioned in 'Touch and talk'.

■ The Allabout sheet for this outline is on page 78.

■ MILK & DAIRY PRODUCTS

■ **BIBLE LINK: 1 Samuel 17:12-22.**
■ **Focus for children:** God provides our food.
■ **Focus for adults:** stress that God is a loving Father who provides for us.

Touch and talk

Bring in a selection of dairy products or their containers – milk bottles/cartons, yoghurt, fromage frais, hard cheese, soft cheese, cottage cheese, and butter, cream, even a can of evaporated milk, and some powdered dried milk. Perhaps provide small cubes of a mild cheese for the children to nibble – but check with adults first as cow's milk allergies are very common in under-fives. Ask the children if they know what cheese is made from. They may not know that everything displayed comes from milk, but will probably know that milk comes from cows.

• Ask them how they get their milk: does the milkman bring it and leave it on the doorstep? In bottles or cartons? What do we use milk for? Many children may drink it, others may have it on breakfast cereals, and may know that adults like it in tea or coffee.

• Ask who likes yoghurt, and what flavours; what about fromage frais? Cream? (Not many children like it.)

• Who likes cheese? How? In sandwiches? Cheese on toast? Grated? Today most of us eat quite a lot of cheese, and we probably buy it every week, but in Bible times cheese was something really special… at this point, to lead in to the story you could produce a piece of cheese, gift-wrapped, looking like a present, which you unwrap as you say the next sentence. 'In fact, if you wanted to give someone important a present you gave him some – cheese!'

Story presentation

You could tell the story like this:

David was the youngest in his family; he had seven big brothers – that's a lot isn't it? 1, 2, 3, 4, 5, 6, 7 big brothers! The three biggest brothers were soldiers; they were in the king's army and they were away from home, fighting. David

stayed at home and looked after his father's sheep. He was a shepherd boy. David's soldier brothers had been away for a long time in the army, and their dad wanted to know how they were getting on; there were no postmen in those days, so he couldn't write a letter; there were no telephones either, so he couldn't phone up. What could he do? He decided to send David to see how they were getting on. He wanted to send them a present. Perhaps the food in the army wasn't very good, so he got ready ten loaves of lovely fresh bread; he also got a big bagful of roasted wheat – a bit like popcorn – for them.
'Now,' thought their dad, 'what can I send to the commander of the soldiers? He's a very important person; it must be a very special present. I know – I'll send some cheese!' That seems a funny present to us doesn't it? We usually have cheese made out of cows' milk, but these cheeses were probably made from goats' milk. (*If possible, show a picture of a whole cheese, eg from a magazine advertisement, or a small complete Dutch cheese.*) The cheeses were very big and round – like this, and David had to take ten of them! And the loaves of bread! And a bag of corn! How could he carry all that? I expect he took a donkey to carry the food, and walked along beside it himself. I expect everyone was pleased to see him, don't you? I hope the commander liked the cheese!

■ ACTIVITIES
Creative prayer-time

Explain that God loves to hear us sing so you are going to sing a prayer to say thank you for milk etc. (Use shakers and the tune 'Frere Jacques'.)
The leader sings the first phrase, perhaps holding up a picture, and the children the second.

Milk and butter (Milk and butter)
Cream and cheese (Cream and cheese)
Fromage frais and yoghurt (Fromage frais and yoghurt)
God made these! (God made these!)

Milk for cornflakes (Milk for cornflakes)
Cheese for tea (Cheese for tea)
Yoghurt for my pudding (Yoghurt for my pudding)
God gives me! (God gives me!)

Lovely chocolate (Lovely chocolate)
Milkshakes too (Milkshakes too)
I like bread and butter (I like bread and butter)
God – thank you! (God – thank you!)

Visual display

Make a huge outline of a cow and write on it 'God gives us milk.' Let the children stick on pictures of dairy products cut from magazines, or cut out sugar-paper shapes of things to do with milk.

Matching activity

Give each child a sheet of paper (A4 or larger) on which are outlined three or four shapes asociated with milk, eg a yoghurt pot, a bar of chocolate, a cream cheese triangle, a milk jug. Provide also a selection of corresponding cut out shapes in different coloured paper. Let children select shapes and glue them to the correct outline.

Wax-resist surprise pictures

Prepare beforehand for each child one or more pieces of white paper on which you have drawn with a white wax crayon or a white household candle a simple outline of something related to today's topic – a milk bottle, a cow, a glass of milk, a piece of cheese. The children choose a piece of paper and then colour the paper with a light colour wash to discover the picture. (They may wish to do more than one so it would be a good idea to keep the categories separate.)

Milk-bottle tops collage

Prepare a simple outline of say a milk bottle or a cow and let children stick on milk-bottle tops to make a picture.

■ SONGS AND RHYMES
* Bottles of milk FFTB 60
God provides LJI 18

■ The Allabout sheet for this outline is on page 79.

■ FRUIT & VEGETABLES

■ **BIBLE LINK: Leviticus 23:39-43.**
■ **Background:** the feast of tabernacles, or 'ingathering', was an important pilgrimage-festival which took place at the end of harvest when all was safely 'gathered in'. The feast lasted eight days and the Bible suggests it was a very joyful time. This particular feast had an extra 'ingredient': the people lived outside, in 'booths' or shelters of palm and willow branches – a reminder of the years their ancestors spent wandering in the wilderness before reaching the Promised Land, when they lived in tents or 'tabernacles'. One can imagine how much Jewish children would have enjoyed this aspect of the feast, and it would also of course have been a wonderful visual aid of how God had brought them to the Promised Land.
■ **Focus for children:** God provides our food.
■ **Focus for adults:** unless we live in an agricultural community it's easy to forget that our food comes ultimately from God. It's good to be grateful, especially in a world where so many people are barely able to scrape a living from the land and feed their children.

Touch and talk

Bring in a selection of fruits and vegetables. (Give them a good wash in case someone decides to sample them!) Let the children handle them, encouraging them to notice the shapes, colours, smells, and the different skin textures. Cut some in half, to show the lovely patterns inside, eg in a pepper or a cabbage, or an orange cut horizontally. An apple cut horizontally gives a pretty star shape around the pips.

Story presentation

You could present the story like this:

We enjoy looking at and eating all these lovely fruits and vegetables. Probably we buy them from shops, but God made them grow for the farmers; God sent the sun and the rain to help them grow in the earth. In Bible times people used to have a great big party every year when they had finished picking all their fruit, and dug up all their vegetables, and cut all their corn. The party lasted eight days. Everyone was very happy and said thank you to God because they had enough fruit and vegetables, enough food to last them for the whole year till the next harvest. For the children it was even more fun, because the whole family used to camp out for this feast! It was a very hot country, and it didn't rain at that time of the year, so they used to cut down branches of trees and make shelters out of doors; they ate and slept in the shelters, saying thank you to God for all the good things he had given them.

■ ACTIVITIES
Creative prayer-time

Let the children sit or stand in a circle; give each child a fruit or vegetable to hold. Tell them to look at their own and everyone else's while you say thank you to God together.

'Thank you God for all these fruits and vegetables. They smell good; they look good; they feel good; they taste good! Thank you for giving them to us. Amen.'

Potato prints/apple prints

Choose potatoes of a size that under-fives' hands can hold easily. Cut them in half and cut away portions of the cut surface to make a printing block. Provide shallow containers – old saucers or large coffee jar lids, of thick bright paint, and let the children print their designs onto paper – as thick as you can manage. As this is a fairly messy activity, enlist as much help as possible and restrict the group to five or six children at a time. A simpler version of this activity is to use an apple cut in half vertically – no need to 'carve' it.

Fruit bowls

Cut a large semicircle of coloured paper for each child, and stick it onto a larger backing sheet of a contrasting colour, as a fruit bowl. Let children cut out, or choose, fruit shapes in different colours and stick them on to make a bowl of fruit. (An alternative would be for children to colour shapes before sticking them on.) This could be adapted as a group activity for a visual display.

Growing cress

Collect polystyrene trays and provide each child with one. Put blotting paper, cotton wool or a layer of kitchen towel or paper tissues in the bottom of each tray, dampen well and add cress seeds. Older children might like to have their initials in cress. Let the children take them home and remind them to keep them watered! Even more fun are 'cress-heads' – see page 14.

■ SONGS AND RHYMES

* Do you plant your cabbages? TLP 85
* God provides LJI 15
* The apple tree RRG 11; TLP 46
* Five fat peas RRG 29
* The cherry tree RRG 46 or TLP 46
* Old Tom Tomato TLP 45
* Five bananas FFTB 180

■ The Allabout sheet for this outline is on page 79.

■ FAMILIES

■ **BIBLE LINK: Luke 4:38 and 39.**
■ **Focus for children:** to help them appreciate the benefits of belonging to an earthly family and to God's family.
■ **Focus for adults:** Jesus is still concerned for every member of our families – young and old.

Touch and talk

Bring in some of your own family photos, or have everyone bring in photos of their families. Show your own and talk to the children about them. You could also show them something that you've inherited (say a watch or a ring), saying something like, 'This brooch is very old and very special; it used to belong to my granny, and now it's mine. It's been in our family a very long time.' Ask how many of them have grannies/uncles/cousins; say that all these people belong to our families. God gives us families so we can look after each other and have fun together. (If any in your group are from reconstituted families, or you have children who are with foster-parents or minders, choose your remarks carefully.)

Story presentation

You could present the story like this:

One day Jesus went to lunch with Peter one of his friends. Granny lived with Peter's family, and she was feeling very poorly that day – in fact she'd stayed in bed instead of getting up and helping. They told Jesus that Granny wasn't well, and Jesus went to see her and made her better! Maybe the family wanted her to sit down quietly for a little while, but Granny said 'No! I feel fine. I'm going to help now.' And she did.

■ ACTIVITIES
Creative prayer-time/visual display

Let each child draw a self-portrait. Stick the portraits, with names, on to a display sheet, headed, 'We all belong to the Jesus family'. As you are sticking on the pictures, sing together 'Belonging to the Jesus family', LJI 98. (This will go to the tune 'Frère Jacques' if you don't feel able to teach the children a new tune.)

My family

Let each child draw – or stick on pre-cut outlines of, and colour – the members of their families. Some children may have a mum, dad, and a sister or brother. Others may have just one parent, but could choose another cut-out for another adult – granny or uncle for example. If wished, an adult could write names or 'titles' on for the children.

Make a card

Give children thick paper or thin card folded into a greetings card shape. On the front should be written (and read to the children) 'To my family' and inside 'I love you, from…' Children linked with more than one family, eg through their parents' divorce, should be encouraged to make more than one card. Provide materials for decorating a card – perhaps circles of tissue paper to make flowers, perhaps a cut-out stem and leaves to be stuck on with a flower-shape on top. Otherwise children could stick on suitable pictures cut from old cards, and maybe embellish these with glitter. Help children to sign their names – even by doing dots for them to write over.

Make a family!

This will take a little advance preparation, but would be enjoyed by the children. Draw some simple animal or insect or fish shapes in varying sizes (maybe with different coloured paper) and help children select a mother and father and two or three children to stick on to a sheet of paper (and colour if necessary). Label their work, 'The fish family' etc.

Play corner

Provide a 'home corner' with plenty of dolls and soft toys, dressing up clothes and, if possible, baby equipment. Let the children 'play' families.

■ SONGS AND RHYMES

Belonging to the Jesus family LJI 98
Caring hands LJI 99
* Here are Grandma's spectacles RRG 23; TLP 35
'Thank you for my family': to the tune, 'Stand up, clap hands' JP 225

Stand up clap hands, shout 'Thank you, Lord,
Thank you for my family!'
Stand up, clap hands, shout 'Thank you, Lord,
For people who belong to me.'
I look around at my mum and my dad,
My brothers and sisters and I'm so glad,
That God has given them all to me,
To love and be part of my family!
(*repeat first verse*)

If several children in your group have experienced the break-up of their families you may prefer this version of 'Thank you for my family'.

Stand up, clap hands, shout, 'Thank you, Lord,
For people who look after me!'
Stand up, clap hands, shout, 'Thank you, Lord,
I'm part of your family!'

When I look round at the people who care,
For me and my friends, I'm glad we can share,
The wonderful world God's given to me –
I'm glad to be part of God's family!

Stand up, clap hands, shout, 'Thank you, Lord,
For people who look after me!'
Stand up, clap hands, shout, 'Thank you, Lord,
I'm part of your family!'

'Sing a song of families': to the tune: 'Sing a song of sixpence'

Sing a song of families,
Brothers, sisters too.
Uncles, aunties, cousins,
How many have you?

Grannies, grandads, parents,
Here or far away,
Thank you for our families,
Please bless them all today.

■ The Allabout sheet for this outline is on page 80.

■ MUSIC

■ **BIBLE LINK: Psalm 150 and 2 Chronicles 5 – the dedication of the temple.**

■ **Background:** the tribe of Levi were involved in worship from the time of Moses. In Solomon's day they were the official musicians, leading the praise and worship with singing and musical instruments.

■ **Focus for children:** to involve the children in creating music and sounds as part of their worship.

■ **Focus for adults:** music is a precious gift from God and can be used as an aid to quiet meditative prayer as well as in joyful praise.

Touch and talk

• Have a tape of worship songs for children playing at the beginning of your time together today.

• Talk about when they hear music – on television... in church... at home? What is their favourite music? What are their favourite songs at church? Perhaps some of them have members of their family who play musical instruments? Have a selection of instruments available to show the children. Include some simple instruments that they can experiment with – drums, cymbals, tambourines, bells, castanets, recorders etc. (Your local school might be able to lend you some, if you ask them.) If possible, have some more 'sophisticated' instruments as well. Perhaps some of the adults present can play instruments and would be willing to demonstrate?

Show how the instruments are played – eg blown, hit, bowed. Let the children experiment with the percussion instruments; see how many different sounds they can make!

Story presentation

If possible, lead into the story by making some musical instruments (as described on page 15). Otherwise have some percussion instruments available for the children to play during the course of the story. You could use the singing of songs in prayer or worship (as outlined below) in the dramatisation of the story. (See 'God gives us Fish' for an approach to dramatisation.)

You will need one child to be

Solomon and the rest to be his musicians. If you are able to have everyone dress up, so much the better.

Take the children to the back and expain that until King Solomon organised the building of the temple, the people had no proper building where they could worship God. Solomon had made the temple as beautiful as possible and today it was finished. Explain that Solomon and all the people had come to worship God in it for the first time. Try to help the children feel as if they are really there: perhaps you could use the parents present as 'the people', all waiting quietly for the worship to begin.

Give each child (except Solomon) an instrument. Walk to the front in a procession led by Solomon, the children playing their instruments and shouting, 'Praise the Lord!' When you get to the front of the church, sing one or two lively songs which the children can accompany with their instruments. Explain to the children that when the people did this, God was so pleased with their singing and praise that he filled the whole temple with a cloud, to show them that he was there with them, listening to their worship.

Singing to God

Let the children choose their favourite songs and sing them all together to God. Don't discourage the children from choosing 'secular' songs. 'Humpty Dumpty' is as much an offering of worship to a small child as a 'Christian' song is. The important thing is that they are singing *to* God and are reassured that he is interested in their world. Include some action songs, too.

■ ACTIVITIES
Creative prayer-time

• This prayer 'makes a joyful noise to the Lord.' Give each child an instrument and ask them to hold it very still, until the end of the prayer when the children play their instruments as loudly as possible.

Thank you, God, for music to enjoy:
To listen to and to play.
Thank you that you like us to sing to you:
Thank you that we can praise you with our instruments.
WE PRAISE YOU!

• 'Lord, we've come to worship You' – IFW 56 – is a song which can be sung as a quiet prayer.

Visual display

Collect as many 'musical' pictures as you can. Cut out an A4 sized outline of a church building from coloured card. Help the children to make their collage by sticking on pictures to cover the outline.

Stick all the collages on to a large piece of lining paper (or coloured sugar paper) to make a frieze. Write the words: 'Thank you, Lord, for music to play...right where we are.'

Musical games

Prepare a tape of a selection of different kinds of music – TV themes, pop songs, nursery rhymes, songs from church, advertising jingles etc. See how many of them the children can identify.

See page 15 for more ideas for musical games.

Musical instruments

See page 15 for ideas on how to make musical instruments.

Musical mobile

In advance, draw simple outlines of musical instruments on pieces of card. Help the children to cut out the shapes and to punch a hole in the top of each one. Let them choose shapes for their mobile, and give them each a strip of card with the words, 'We praise God with music.' Help them to attach their musical instruments to the strip of card with thread.

■ SONGS AND RHYMES

* The music man OTU 44
* Let us praise the Lord with guitar CH 105
* God is our Father SHF 132; CH 109
We'll praise him on the trumpet IFW 91
* I will show you I'm rejoicing IFW 42

■ The Allabout sheet for this outline is on page 80.

■ ANIMALS TO CARE FOR

■ **BIBLE LINK: Psalm 23 and 1 Samuel 17:34-36 – David's care for his sheep.**

■ **Focus for children:** to increase children's awareness of animals and the natural world, and to encourage care for them.

■ **Focus for adults:** we are responsible for the wildlife on our planet. God gave us dominion over animals – not for exploitation, but for stewardship. If we allow a species to become extinct we are not exercising that stewardship responsibly.

Touch and talk

Find pictures of pets and show them to the group. Encourage the children to talk about their pets and how they help to look after them. What do they eat? Where do they sleep?

If it's practical, take some small animals for them to see. *Do make sure they are very securely caged* as young children are fascinated by small animals and are likely to try to take them out to stroke. Watch, too, for poking fingers.

Story presentation

This lends itself well to a leader taking the part of David and the children being sheep. Narrate the story as if you are David telling someone else how you care for your sheep. Encourage the children to follow the 'stage directions' in your story – perhaps another leader, or willing mum, would help out. (See the outline on 'Fish', page 44, for more instructions for this type of story telling.) A simple sling made out of brown material would add to the story. You may wish to cover the following points.

• Tell your 'friend' how you (David) would care for your sheep during the day. You'd take the sheep out, looking for the sweetest grass there was. (*Children follow on hands and knees.*)

• Talk about how you would play your harp and sing songs to God while the sheep were eating the grass. (*Children pretend to graze.*)

• Say that you would find pools of fresh water for the sheep to drink so that they wouldn't be thirsty. (*Children follow again, then pretend to drink.*)

• Show how you would search for any sheep that got lost and how pleased you'd be when you found them. Explain how you would carry the youngest lambs if they got tired. (*Pick up one of the smallest children whom you know well.*)

• Talk about taking the sheep back to the sheepfold and showing them inside where they'd be safe for the night. Show how you would sleep across the doorway so that you would be close to them all night. (*Huddle the 'sheep' into a corner, to serve as a sheepfold and sit or lie down in front of them.*)

• If a wolf or bear attacked, tell your friend, you would be ready to fight them. (*Look around, as if on guard, and have your sling ready.*)

• Conclude by saying that you always look after your sheep very well because you care about each one. You want them all to be well and safe and happy.

■ ACTIVITIES

Creative prayer-time

This prayer should be started in a whisper, and the volume increased as the animals get bigger! Everyone joins in the words in italics.

For little furry animals,
We thank you, Lord.
For hamsters, mice and gerbils,
We thank you, Lord.
For swimming fish and singing birds,
We thank you, Lord.
For cats and dogs and rabbits,
We thank you, Lord.
For horses, cows and elephants,
We thank you, Lord.
For all your creatures, big and small,
We thank you, Lord.

Pairing game

Make a collection of animal pictures, pictures of the sort of food they eat and pictures of the homes they live in. Display the pictures of animals. Put the pictures of homes and food into a bag. Let the children take turns to draw out a picture from the bag and see if they can match it up with the correct animal. Have as wide a range of animals as possible, including wild animals and zoo animals.

Visual display

Make a frieze of endangered species. On a large sheet of paper (lining paper) write: 'These are the animals you made, God. Please help us to take care of them.' Help the children to stick on pictures of wild animals, including as many endangered species as possible, and talk about the animals as you do so. How many of the animals can the children recognise?

Make a furry rabbit

Have ready some scraps of fur fabric, in different colours if possible. Give each child a piece of thin card on which has been drawn a bold outline of a rabbit (or cat). Help the children to stick on the pieces of fabric, trimmed if necessary, to make their furry animal. They might like to give it a name, which an adult could write underneath. Alternatively, you could cut the rabbit shapes out and write the rabbit's name on the back.

Model some strange animals

Give the children some playdough, and let them make some strange animals. Encourage their creativity and they will come up with some very odd species! Display them safely until it's time to go home.

Storytime

Read the story *Dear Zoo* by Rod Campbell (Bodley Head). The children will enjoy making the noises of the animals!

■ SONGS AND RHYMES

* The butterfly song CSM 27 or JP 54

Thank you, Lord, for... dogs to pat,
.... cats to stroke,
... birds that sing,
... lions that roar,
... cows to milk.
(to the tune, 'Thank you, Lord, for this fine day')

* The animal fair OTU 11
* Animal playtime FFTB 129
* Lazy lambs FFTB 132
* A little brown rabbit TLP 151
God was with David LJI 37

■ The Allabout sheet for this outline is on page 81.

■ HOMES

■ **BIBLE LINK: The wise and foolish builders – Matthew 7:24-27.**
■ **Focus for children:** God provides us with our homes.
■ **Focus for adults:** Jesus warns of the dangers of building our lives on insecure foundations. If we live according to his teaching, in his power, we shall be secure.

Touch and talk

Bring in pictures of different kinds of houses – your own, and perhaps an igloo, a mud hut, a flat-roofed house, a teepee or other tent and a palace, as well as different types of house found in your area. Ask the children about the pictures: what are houses made from in this country, and in other countries? Ask about their own houses. Have they got gardens? Chimneys? Doorbells? Stairs? How are our houses different from those of people living in other countries? Say Jesus told a story about two houses.

Story presentation

Instead of telling the story in your own words you might like to use the form given in LJI 76-77.

■ ACTIVITIES
Creative prayer-time/visual display

On a large display sheet outline a house, with enough brick shapes for each child in the group to colour one in. Head the sheet, 'God gives us our homes'. Give each child a brick shape to colour and, if they are able, let them write their names; otherwise let a helper do it for them. Let the children come in turn to stick their bricks on the house, perhaps during other activities. Pray briefly and simply with each child, thanking God for their homes and asking him to bless them.

Alternatively, give each child a house shape and let them draw in windows and doors so that it looks like their own house (to them anyway!). If some in your group live in blocks of flats provide rectangles of paper as well as traditional shapes with pointed roofs. Display all the houses as a long street or all together like a town seen from a hill. Label the display 'These are our houses; thank you God for our homes.' The *Lion Book of Children's Prayers* has prayers about homes.

Houses

You may already have a 'home corner'; if not, improvise with sturdy tables covered with old sheets, or borrow a couple of 'Wendy houses'. Add a few dressing-up clothes and pots and pans and let children dress up and 'play house'. Some children might prefer to build houses from Duplo, Lego or wooden building blocks.

Other people's homes

Help children make:
• flat roofed houses from shoe boxes – you will need to cut windows, or they could draw them on or use sticky paper;
• igloos – stick cotton wool onto 2D igloo shapes;
• teepees – practise this one first; it's not difficult once you've got the hang of it! For each teepee you need three plastic drinking straws and something (eg a plastic coated 'freezer tie') to tie them at the top to form a triangular 'frame', a semicircle of paper, and a stapler. Let the children decorate the semicircles (felt tips, sticky shapes etc) before you form each one into a cone and staple the outside edges together at the bottom. Slip this over the 'frame' made by the straws. A simpler, but slightly less authentic looking teepee could be made from decorated cones of card.

'Look inside' houses

Cut 'house' shapes from pieces of paper folded like greetings cards. Show children how to draw windows and a door on the front, then open up and let them draw what's inside the house, or stick in pictures from mail order catalogues.

■ SONGS AND RHYMES

* The wise man built his house upon the rock JP 252
God provides LJI 15
The old house FFTB 58
* Building FFTB 80
Do you know where you live? FFTB 81
* Here is a house TLP 25; 27
* My little house TLP 29
* Build a house with five bricks TLP 32
* My house RRG 14

■ The Allabout sheet for this outline is on page 81.

◼ CLOTHES

◼ **BIBLE LINK: Acts 9:36-40.**
◼ **Focus for children:** God provides us with clothes to wear.
◼ **Focus for adults:** Dorcas was involved in her community – and her practical kindness was important enough to be mentioned in the Bible. God appreciates the kindness we show to others and our involvement in our community.

Touch and talk

If you feel adventurous you could appear in something wildly inappropriate, like your night-clothes and dressing gown or your swimming things. Ask the children if they can see anything different about you and lead on to a discussion about clothes. Alternatively, have a selection of dressing-up clothes for the children to try on – remember to include a variety of hats. Try also to have some unusual clothes – perhaps from a different culture – or some postcards of people in national costume. Give children time to look at and handle these things, then talk about clothes using perhaps one of the following lines of thought:
• Why do we wear clothes?
• People who wear uniforms.
• Special clothes for special jobs: aprons; overalls; white coats.
• Special clothes for special days and activities: wedding dresses; party clothes; 'best' clothes.

Story presentation 1

It's unnecessary to describe the miracle of Dorcas being brought back to life. Simply tell the story of a lady who was good at sewing and made clothes for other people. You could lead into this by asking where the children get their clothes – shops, jumble/nearly new sales, passed on from bigger brothers and sisters or cousins? Say that sometimes our mums or aunties or friends who are good at sewing or knitting make things for us, and there's a story in the Bible about a lady like that.

Story presentation 2

An alternative to telling the story of Dorcas would be to use the story 'Timmy's new jumper', which follows. (You need several props for this story – including the sheep mask shown – and

it's a good idea to practise in front of a mirror a few times, so that the pace is maintained. It's designed to show children that God gives us our clothes; this is not so obvious to them as God giving us food, so it's good to demonstrate visually.) If you can't act it out, try telling it with the help of a few simple pictures cut from magazines.

Timmy had a new jumper (*show child's hand-knitted jumper*). His Granny had made it for his birthday;

Timmy went to say thank you to Granny (*put on glasses and shawl for Granny*). 'Thank you for my lovely jumper, Granny,' said Timmy. 'Oh,' said Granny, '**I** only knitted it with wool from the wool shop. You'd better thank the lady in the wool shop.'

Timmy went to see the lady in the wool shop (*take off shawl and glasses and put on hat*). 'Thank you for the lovely jumper that Granny knitted me,' said Timmy. 'Oh,' said the lady in the wool shop, 'Don't thank **me**; I only sold the wool. The wool came from a sheep; you need to say thank you to the sheep.'

Timmy found a sheep (*put on sheep mask and/or sheepskin rug*) and said, 'Thank you for the wool for my lovely jumper.' 'Don't thank **me**,' said the sheep, 'The grass I eat helps me grow my woolly coat; you'd better thank the grass.' (*Take off sheep disguise.*)

Timmy knelt down and said thank you to the grass. 'Don't thank **me**,' said the grass, 'The sun and the rain help me grow. Thank them' (*hold up umbrella and yellow disc*).

'Thank you, sun and rain, for making the grass grow so the sheep can grow the wool for my lovely new jumper,' said Timmy. 'Don't thank **us**,' said the sun and the rain, '**We** only do what God tells us to do; thank God.'

So Timmy found out where his lovely new jumper had come from.
Granny knitted it with wool;
the wool came from a shop;
the lady in the shop got the wool from a sheep;
the sheep ate grass to grow a woolly coat;
the sun and the rain helped the grass to grow;
God sent the sun and the rain;
– so God as well as Granny made Timmy's jumper!

◼ ACTIVITIES
Creative prayer-time/visual display

Make a large poster with the caption: 'God gives us clothes to wear.' Let the children stick on pictures of clothes. As they do so, thank God for that particular category of clothes.

Clothes-lines

Provide each child with a piece of paper on which is drawn a washing line between two posts. Let them cut out pictures of clothes from old catalogues and stick them on the washing line. (If no catalogues are available, provide simple clothes shapes – a T shirt, trousers, long socks – which the children could colour before gluing on.) This could be adapted as an activity prayer with each child putting one item on the line, and saying thank you for clothes.

Dressing up

Provide old clothes for the children to dress up in. Include safe beads, bangles, handbags, hats and shoes as often these accessories are the most popular. Try to bring a mirror for them to admire the effect!

Sorting socks

Older children would enjoy sorting out pairs of socks (they need to be fairly obvious – bright colours or striking patterns) and matching them.

Clothes montage

Give each child a simple outline of a dress or a coat or a pair of trousers and let them stick on small pieces of brightly coloured material.

◼ SONGS AND RHYMES
* Doing the washing FFTB 64
* Mother's washing TLP 34 (slightly dated now as it talks about washing by hand, but fun all the same)
Baa baa black sheep (traditional)

◼ The Allabout sheet for this outline is on page 82.

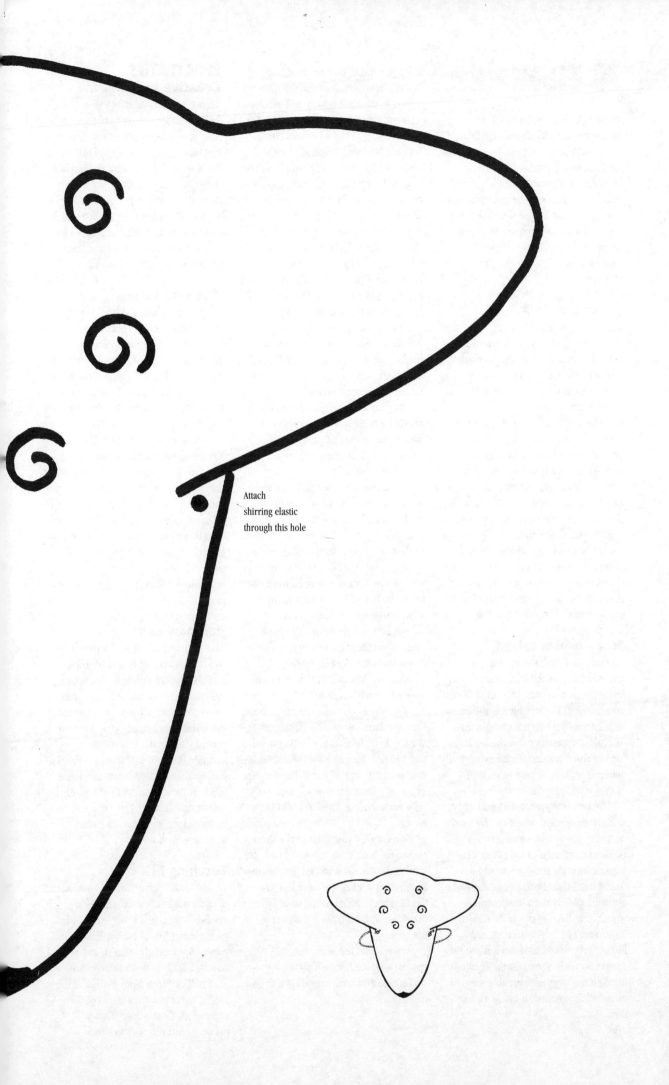

Attach
shirring elastic
through this hole

■ FISH

■ **BIBLE LINK: John 21:1-14.**
■ **Focus for children:** to help understand that God provides us with food, including fish.
■ **Focus for adults:** Jesus understood perfectly the disciples' needs – to have something to show for a night's fishing, and a good hot breakfast. He understands our needs too – emotional and physical as well as spiritual.

Touch and talk

If possible, have goldfish for the children to look at. Encourage them to describe what they can see. Explain that the fish can 'breathe' underwater.

A herring-sized fish from the fishmonger makes a good visual aid. You can show the children the different parts of its body – especially its gills – and let them feel its scaly skin if they want to. Alternatively you could take pictures of fish that we eat, tins of fish, or a fish-finger packet, as this is likely to be the form in which most young children eat fish. Some pictures of fishing boats of various kinds would also be suitable. Talk to them about the things you've brought in, and find out if they like fish and if they know where it comes from.

Story presentation

One way of telling a story is by encouraging the children to act it out, but instead of having different children take different parts (which is difficult with under-fives) all the children are disciples. Remember that the leader's tone of voice and facial expression will generate an atmosphere to which the children will respond.

Use very few props; cushions or shallow cardboard boxes can be used as boats. Try to find some pictures of Galilean fishermen casting their nets. Explain how the disciples would have fished from their boats at night. Draw out from the children how exciting it would have been to catch the fish, and how tired, cold, disappointed and hungry they would have been when they caught nothing. Then talk the children through the story encouraging them to mime all the actions. It could go like this:

Let's pretend to be friends of Jesus. We're feeling very sad because he seems to have gone away and we don't know when we'll see him again. We've decided to go fishing, so let's climb into the boat and row it out into the sea. It's night-time. Let's get hold of the nets and throw them over the edge of the boat into the water. Ready? Throw! Listen to them go 'plop' as they hit the water. Now we have to wait a while, sitting quite still in the boat.

It's time to see whether we've caught any fish. We'll pull in the nets to see if they're heavy. No? Oh dear, we'll have to haul the nets in and try again.

Let's try the other side of the boat this time... Still nothing? We'll have to haul in our nets again (Depending on the response of your group, you can repeat this several times.)

We've been fishing for hours and it's nearly morning now. We'd better row back to shore. Aren't we cold? And we're tired and hungry and we haven't caught any fish at all.

Just a moment, though, there's someone on the beach waving to us. He's shouting, 'Have you caught any fish?' What shall we tell him? We'll have to shout back, 'No! Nothing.'

The man's shouting something else now. What? Try once again? Doesn't he know the fish will all have gone by now? It's no use fishing in daylight!

But he's still shouting, 'Put your nets out on the right side of the boat. There will be some fish there.'

Shall we? Yes, we will, but I'm sure we won't catch anything.

We'll throw our nets out of the boat one last time... But wait a minute! What's this? The nets are getting heavier and heavier. We can't hold them. Mind you don't fall in! Pull hard! The nets are breaking, there are so many fish. Let's help each other get the nets into the boat.

Now quickly row back to the shore before the boat sinks. Do you know, I think I've guessed who that man on the beach is? It's Jesus! He's made a fire on the beach and he's inviting us to have breakfast with him. We'll leap out of the boat.

'Bring some fish with you,' he shouts. 'And we'll have a picnic.'

Let's go and have breakfast with Jesus.

■ ACTIVITIES
Creative prayer-time

Use a large net (from the greengrocer) or an old piece of green plastic garden netting to make a prayer net. Give each child a fish shape cut out of thin card. Ask the children to think of someone/ something they want to tell Jesus about and help them to write their prayer on the fish. The children can then put their fish into the nets, which can then be fastened on to the wall of the church or the room where the group meets.

A sea-bed frieze

A very attractive sea picture can be made using large sheets of sandpaper for the sand, with a dark blue strip above this for the sea and a lighter blue for the sky. (Or you could colour wash a piece of ready-pasted wallpaper and let the children sprinkle sand along the bottom.)

Strips of green tissue of different shades make strands of seaweed, which can then be attached at just one end, so that they hang loose. Give the children some grey shapes for rocks, and lots of different sorts of cut-out fish to stick on. (Ready-pasted paper makes it easy to stick shapes on. Try sticking on some tiny sea-shells, too.)

Write in the sky: 'God gives us fish to eat.'

Rainbow fish

Give each child a large, simple outline of a fish, cut out of thin card. Have available lots of pulses – red, brown and green lentils, red and white beans, mung beans, chick peas, etc. (Never use red kidney beans.) Help them to spread glue on the fish and then sprinkle the pulses in vertical stripes to give a rainbow effect. Choose a large bean for the eye, or let the children colour one in. (The very youngest children may try to eat the beans, so keep an eye on them!)

Catching fish

You will need: some 'fishing rods' made of small magnets ('Polo' shapes are easiest), string, and short lengths of garden cane; lots of cut-out fish with paper clips on their mouths; and several boxes or buckets to serve as 'ponds'.

Small children enjoy fishing in the boxes, which requires little co-ordination. Close supervision is needed, however, with the rods.

Matchbox boats

You will need one matchbox for each child. Remove the lid and place a blob of Plasticine in the base of each box; let the children decorate the top surface of the lid with paints, felt tips or coloured gummed paper. Cut a sail from strong paper or thin card (decorate it if time allows) and thread a cocktail stick through the sail; replace the matchbox lid and push the cocktail stick sail through it into the Plasticine in the base of the box. Add a small piece of Plasticine to the sharp end of the cocktail stick.

■ SONGS AND RHYMES

* Peter and James and John in a sailboat JP 197; CH 101
* Andrew, Andrew (adapted for Peter) LJI 64
* I love to row in my big blue boat TLP 111
* One, two, three four five TLP 112
* Here is the sea, the wavy sea TLP 112

■ The Allabout sheet for this outline is on page 82.

■ FRIENDS

■ **BIBLE LINK: David and Jonathan – 1 Samuel 18-20.**
■ **Focus for children:** children of this age are just beginning to socialise. This session is a chance to explore what friendship is and to begin to lay the foundations for friendship with God.
■ **Focus for adults:** David and Jonathan's friendship is probably the best known friendship in the Bible. It emphasises a basic need – to be loved and accepted by someone else. It is important to give ourselves enough time to make and keep friends. God offers us lasting friendship, total acceptance and unchanging love. He will never 'move away' and leave us, and he offers forgiveness and healing.

Touch and talk

If it's possible, the leader should bring a friend who doesn't normally come to the group and introduce him/her to the children. Talk about your friendship – what you do together, how you met, what you have in common, etc. Encourage the children to ask questions and to find out about your friend.

Talk about their friendships in a similar way; what are the names of their friends? Where do they meet them? What do they do together? What are their favourite games? Are there any special friendships within the group?

Talk about falling out and quarrelling. What happens when they get cross with each other? How do they make friends again?

(Remember that the younger children are still at the stage of playing alongside rather than *with* their friends, but enjoy the companionship of others their own age, nonetheless.)

Story presentation

You could use simple puppets to tell the story. Emphasise David and Jonathan's friendship – who they were, what they did together, the love they had for each other. For an abridged version of this part of 1 Samuel, also with a 'Friendship' theme, see *The Lion Book of Bible Stories and Prayers*, no. 14.

■ ACTIVITIES
Creative prayer-time

• Have ready OHP acetates or clearly drawn pictures of friends (having fun; falling out; making up; David and Jonathan) to show during this prayer.

Thank you, Lord, for our friends.
Thank you that we can play together and enjoy one another's toys.
Sometimes we quarrel or fight.
Please help us not to stay cross for long.
Please help us to care for our friends, like Jonathan cared for David.

• Sing 'Jesus loves Kristi' (FS 83) as a prayer, putting in the names of the children's special friends, instead of Kristi. Finish with.'Jesus, Jesus loves all of us.'

Linked hands

Make up some thick powder paint in one or two different colours. Draw a circle on a large sheet of paper (eg lining paper) to act as a rough guide. Help the children to make handprints round the circle, slightly overlapping if possible, to suggest linked hands. Inside the circle, write the words: 'Friends play together,' or 'God gives us friends to play with.'

Any left-over paint can be used to make handprint pictures to take home.

Have lots of soapy water and towels ready! If you can, warn parents in advance so that they can dress the children in play clothes. Plastic aprons or old shirts are useful to protect clothes.

Doing together – iced biscuits

Take some plain biscuits to the group, some made-up glacé icing, and some hundreds and thousands. Help the children to decorate the biscuits, which later will be shared with everyone – perhaps with a drink. Make sure you have plenty for everyone!

Choosing together – a singing game

Play a 'choosing' game, like 'The farmer's in his den.' Play it several times to allow as many children as possible to participate. (Some children may be very dominant, others very shy.

Involving mums and dads may help to give some confidence to the quieter ones.)

Play a game that links hands, like 'Ring-o, ring-o roses,' or 'Here we go round the mulberry bush'.

Sharing together – sweets

Share some sweets, crisps or raisins among the group. You could do this by encouraging the children to sit in a circle and pass the bowl (of sweets etc) to one another. Keep a watchful eye for the child who tries to hold on to it or take more than his/her share. If this happens – as it probably will! – explain gently that they are *sharing* with each other, so everyone has some. This can become a real learning point for some children.

Paper friends

Although young children find cutting out difficult, the results of this activity give so much pleasure to little ones that it is worth the time and effort helping them to do it.

For each set of dolls you will need a piece of coloured paper about 30 x 10 cm (a sheet of A4 cut in half lengthways will do very well). Fold the sheet in half and then into three as shown. Draw a simple gingerbread person on the folded sheet, making sure that the arms go right to the edge of the paper. Cut along the lines. When you open out the paper, the dolls will all be holding hands.

The children will need a great deal of assistance with this activity, so it is a good idea to ask parents to help. They will probably like to colour the dolls, and older children can be helped to write, 'Thank you, God, for our friends,' on them.

■ SONGS AND RHYMES

* Let everyone clap hands with me
  OTU 2
Jesus is a friend of mine JP 136
God is pleased when we are friends
  CSM 32
I rejoice in making Jesus happy IFW 37
'Jesus loves us' can be sung to the tune 'Yellow submarine' and accompanied with simple percussion instruments.

Chorus
Jesus loves us, he's our special friend,
He's our special friend, he's our
   special friend.
Jesus loves us, he's our special friend,
He's our special friend, he's our
   special friend.

He was born in Bethlehem,
Angels sang, shepherds came.
Loved the children, everyone,
Everyone can be his friend.

(*Chorus*)

So we sing our praise to him,
Wave our hands, dance for joy.
For he loves us, everyone,
Young and old, girl and boy.

(*Chorus*)

■ The Allabout sheet for this outline is on page 83.

■ PEOPLE WHO NEED OUR HELP

■ **BIBLE LINK: 1 Kings 17:8-16 – Elijah and the widow of Zarephath.**

■ **Focus for children:** most small children know what it's like to feel hungry and to look forward to a favourite meal, so even though the stark reality of starvation is too much for them to handle at this age, they can identify with other children who may not have as many enjoyable things in their lives as they do.

■ **Focus for adults:** we are called by God to see beyond our comfortable lifestyle, and to attend to the needs of those around us. Our children will absorb our values as they grow up and their attitudes to the disadvantaged in our society and in the world will depend to a great extent on our own.

Touch and talk

• Have a selection of different foods available – particularly foods that are likely to be favourites, eg sweets, fruit, crisps, cakes, biscuits, chocolate, bread, etc.

• Talk about their favourite foods: which meals do they most enjoy? What don't they like? What do they do if they don't like something that has been cooked for them?

• Talk about times when they have been hungry – include times when they have been ill and haven't been allowed to eat or haven't wanted to eat. What happens if you don't eat for a long time?

Introduce the idea that not all children have the kinds of foods that they eat. If possible, try to have some special foods from another culture (eg halva) for the children to try, or show some pictures.

• Some children don't have enough to eat – some never have meat, or eggs or fresh fruit. Some children only eat rice or bread or vegetables all the time, and they are very hungry. Let the children try some cooked rice, dry bread, chapatis or pitta bread.

Story presentation

A retelling of the story is set-out below. Find an appropriate picture to go with each paragraph and use them as visual aids.

Elijah loved God and knew that God cared for him. He wanted other people to love God and obey him too.

One day Elijah was very hungry and very hot. The sun shone all the time and there had been no rain for three years. All the plants had died and there was hardly any food for anyone.

Just then he saw an old woman gathering sticks for a fire. 'Would you give me a little water,' he asked her, 'and a little piece of bread?'

The old woman was very kind. She said, 'I don't have enough food for myself and my son, but come and share what we have.' She baked him some bread and invited him to stay with her until the rains came again.

'Don't worry,' said Elijah. 'God will look after us.'

And God did. Elijah stayed with the woman and her son until the rains came and made the plants grow again. In all that time the old woman's jar of flour and bottle of oil didn't run out.

Elijah said Thank you to the old woman for helping him.

They both said Thank you to God for looking after them.

■ ACTIVITIES
Creative prayer-time

Collect lots of pictures of people who need help and people helping others in all kinds of situations – digging wells, building hospitals, mission work, helping children etc. Have a balance of local, national and international scenes. Write at the top of the frieze, 'These people need our help,' and at the bottom, 'Jesus helps us to help them.' Then let the children stick on a selection of the pictures at random. As they do so, talk about the help people are giving. Finish off the prayer-time with a one-sentence prayer about people who need our help.

Baking

Small children love real cooking and it's very easy to make scones or chapatis.

Bowl of rice montage

Using sheets of coloured sugar paper as background, draw a simple bowl shape. Help the children to stick on tiny pieces of overlapping paper, torn from magazines, to cover the bowl. Stick on screwed-up white tissue for the rice, or use real rice, which will stick on with a good PVA adhesive. (If you use real rice, keep a careful eye on the youngest members, who may try to eat it or push it up noses.)

Sand picture

Link this with the story. Give each child a simple pre-drawn picture of a desert scene. Help them to spread PVA glue on the outline and then shake sand onto it. The sand sticks to the glue to make a desert picture. Stick on bits of straw or hay to represent the shrivelled-up plants, and colour in a very bright sun.

Money box

Empty Smartie tubes make good money boxes. Give each child an empty tube and some brightly coloured paper. (Gummed paper squares work well.) Help them to cover their tubes and perhaps decorate them with gummed shapes. Suggest that they use their money boxes to save 1p pieces – a full tube takes about 80p. The money could then be brought to the group and donated to an organisation working for needy children.

■ SONGS AND RHYMES

* He's got the whole wide world in his hands JP 78 – include a verse, 'He's got people needing help in his hands.' Neighbours CH 88
* Father God, you show your care LJI 7

■ The Allabout sheet for this outline is on page 84.

■ PEOPLE WHO CARE FOR US

■ **BIBLE LINK: the book of Ruth.**

■ **Focus for children:** to help the children understand that people other than those in their families love and care for them.

■ **Focus for adults:** the 'significant adults' in a child's world (the adults they meet at the shops, at playgroup, and in the extended family) are important because they widen the child's horizons and help him to build relationships. It is important, therefore, that adults who have such close contact with our children can be trusted to welcome them, affirm them and keep them safe.

Touch and talk

• Ask the children to bring photos of people who are special to them – mums, dads, grandparents, aunts and uncles, childminders, babysitters, etc. (Be sensitive to those children who are children of single parents, broken marriages, melded families etc.) Using the photos as a starting point, encourage the children to talk about the people who care for them. Apart from the family there may be childminders, playgroup leaders, nursery school staff, friends' mums etc.

How often do they see these important people? What do these people do for them? What do they most enjoy doing with these carers?

• Talk about special times – birthdays, family gatherings, bed-times etc. Talk with the children about being co-operative and helpful; use examples to help them understand why it is important to obey rules (like not running into the road) but that they don't have to do what *any* adult tells them.

Story presentation

Use a flannel board or puppets as visual aids for this story.

Naomi lived in a country that wasn't her own. Her husband was dead, but she had two big sons and their wives to take care of her. They were all very happy together.

One awful day Naomi's sons died too, and Naomi and her sons' wives – Orpah and Ruth – were left all alone.

Naomi decided to go back to her own country. Ruth and Orpah started to go with her, to keep her company, but Naomi said No. 'You have been good to me,' she said. 'Stay here, find good husbands and make your homes here.'

Orpah did as Naomi had said, but Ruth wouldn't leave. 'I'm staying with you,' she said. 'I'll go with you wherever you go. You are my family now, and I want to take care of you. I'm coming, too!'

So Ruth and Naomi travelled a long way, back to Naomi's country. Ruth took care of Naomi and was kind to her.

One day, Ruth went to gather some food for them both from some nearby cornfields. There, she met a kind man named Boaz, who owned the fields. Boaz liked Ruth and asked her to marry him. She and Naomi went to live with him in his big house.

Soon Ruth had a baby boy. Naomi was delighted and took care of the baby, just as Ruth had cared for her.

She was thankful to God that he had looked after them all and kept them safe.

■ ACTIVITIES
Creative prayer-time

• Use pictures cut from magazines to represent people who care for the children. On a large piece of coloured paper write, 'Please, God, take care of the people who take care of us,' or, 'Thank you, God, for the people who care for us.'

Help the children to choose and stick the pictures at random on the paper. Place the finished collage on the floor and gather the children round it, perhaps holding hands. Encourage the children to say a prayer for their carers by simply saying their names.

• Draw a prayer. Give each child a piece of paper and some crayons or felt-tip pens. Ask them to draw a picture of the special person/people who care for them and whom they love. Explain to the children that Jesus knows whom they have drawn and he cares for them.

Young children usually like to draw and colour, so even if mummy is a bright red blob, they will enjoy this activity.

Simon says

Remind children that being cared for means that they have to learn to obey certain instructions and keep rules. (Be careful about the language that you use here: it is important not to give the impression that children always have to 'do what grown-ups tell them' because of the danger of abuse.) However, children do have to learn co-operative behaviour. 'Simon says' is a game where the children copy an action or obey an instruction if 'Simon' says, but not otherwise. Eg, 'Simon says, put your hand on your head,' should be obeyed; but the instruction, 'Put your hand on your head,' should not.

Photo frames

Help the children to make photo frames for the photos of their 'special people'. Cut out pieces of card about 16 x 12 cm. Cut a rectangular hole in half the pieces of card to leave a 2 cm border. Help each child stick the border onto the backing on three sides only, to make a simple mount for a photo. Provide crayons or gummed paper shapes so that they can decorate the border. This will take a 13 x 9cm photo. Smaller photos can be glued into the 'window'.

If the children want to, an adult could write on the back, 'Please, God, take care of...' or, 'Thank you, God, for ... who takes care of me.'

Have some pictures of carers available for those children who haven't got photos.

People mobile

For this activity you will need some thin card and pictures of people who can represent the children's carers.

Help the children to choose several pictures and to stick them on to the card. Help them to cut them out, and write on the back of each picture the name of the person the picture represents.

Give each child a ring made from a strip of thick card with the ends stuck together, and some thread. Help the children to suspend the pictures from the ring. Add an extra length of thread to hang up the mobile.

■ SONG AND RHYMES

Thank you Lord, for this fine day CSM 6 – lends itself well to adaptation and can be used for this theme

Who does Jesus love? CH 86
I'm very glad of God SSL 22
* Lollipop Lady FFTB 76
Caring hands LJI 99

■ The Allabout sheet for this outline is on page 84.

PEOPLE JESUS HELPED: 1

■ **BIBLE LINK: John 2:1-10 – the wedding feast at Cana.**

■ **Focus for children:** Jesus is always there, both in the happy times and in the times when we need his help.

■ **Focus for adults:** Jesus was involved with people. He enjoyed being with people and sharing in their lives – as he still does today. He is there to give us help and support when we ask him.

Touch and talk

Have a selection of wedding items to show the children – photographs, pictures from magazines, wedding cake pictures, or even wedding clothes. Have they ever been to a wedding? Some of the children may have been page-boys or bridesmaids at weddings, and may be very willing to talk about it! Ask the children to describe what they can see in the pictures: what are the people wearing? What are they doing? Where do the children think the wedding is taking place?

Talk about all the help needed when someone gets married: people to clean the church and decorate it; people to take the bride and groom to the wedding; people to prepare the food etc.

Talk about wedding customs in different countries and cultures, too.

Story presentation

Involve all the children, choosing two to be the bride and groom. They will enjoy dressing up! Let the 'bride' have a veil made from an old net curtain and the 'groom' have a prayer shawl (tea towel) or similar head covering.

Spread a large cloth or sheet on the floor, and put out biscuits, raisins, crisps etc. for the wedding feast. Have some **weak** juice, in pottery jugs, for the children to drink. (The jugs will later represent the large water pots in the story.)

Tell the story very simply to the children, and let them eat the food as if they are at the wedding. You could tell it something like this:

Jesus was invited to a wedding. Everyone was enjoying themselves when suddenly the servants began to whisper to each other and they looked worried. The wine had run out! There was no more to drink! Jesus wanted to help, so he said to the servants, 'Fill those water jars right to the top with water.' The servants looked even more worried when he said that – they would get into trouble if they served water at a wedding! Anyway, they went to fetch water and began to tip it into the huge water jars, just as Jesus had said. It took a long time, and when they drew out a cupful they found it had become wine. They took a cup to the man in charge of the feast: 'This is wonderful', he said, 'It's the best wine I've ever tasted.' Jesus had turned the water into the very best wine.

At the end of the story, give the children stronger juice to drink, as if it's the better wine that Jesus had made.

■ ACTIVITIES
Creative prayer-time

• **For the difficult times.** Have ready OHP slides or pictures of some of the following situations that small children might meet:

Jesus, you help us when…
…we feel frightened, (eg a large barking dog)
…we have no one to play with, (eg a child alone)
…Mummy (Daddy, Granny etc) shouts at us, (eg an angry adult)
…we feel cross, (eg two children quarrelling)
…we feel sad, (eg a child holding a broken toy)
…we are ill, (eg a child with a rash)
Thank you that you are always with us.

• **For the happy times.** Have a selection of items and pictures of things for a party, eg balloons, streamers, pictures of ice-cream, jellies, sandwiches, biscuits, cakes, invitation, wrapping paper, party hats etc, to make a party collage. Let the children stick them on to a large piece of lining paper with the caption, 'Thank you, Jesus, that you are with us when we are happy.'

• **Celebrate.** Try playing some co-operatve party games, like Hokey Cokey.

Helping hands

Use thick poster paints and let the children make prints of their hands in various colours. Help them to write 'My helping hands' underneath.

Brides and grooms

Give each child an outline of a bride or groom cut from card. Help them to dress them by sticking on wool for hair, small pieces of white material (ready cut) for the bride's dress and black for the groom's suit. Pieces of lace or net will make a veil for the bride. If you have time, they could make bridesmaids as well and take home a set of figures.

■ SONGS, RHYMES AND GAMES

* Poor Jenny sits a-weeping TLP 196
* Jesus is! LJI 60
* My God is so big! CSM 30 or JP 169
* Looby Loo OTU 4
* We all clap hands together TLP 181
* Join in the game OTU 2
* Hokey cokey (traditional)
* God is good to me

God is good to me; (Point upwards; thumbs up sign; point to self)
God is good to me; (Point upwards; thumbs up sign; point to self)
He holds my hand, (Hold hands together)
He helps me stand, (Stand two fingers together on the other hand)
God is good to me. (As line 1)

* Jesus went to a party

Jesus went to a party, (Walk fingers up arm)
He was having a lovely time, (Roll hands over one another and clap)
When someone came to him and said, (Cup hand behind ear, as if listening)
We haven't any wine! (Shake head)
Jesus told the servants, (Mime giving instructions)
'Fill lots of jars so tall.' (Mime filling jars)
But when they drew the water out (Mime dipping a cup into jar and drinking)
It was wine – the best of all! (Rub tummy and smile)

■ The Allabout sheet for this outline is on page 85.

49

■ PEOPLE JESUS HELPED: 2

■ **BIBLE LINK: Matthew 17:24-27** – the fish with the coin in its mouth.

■ **Focus for children:** this outline extends the children's understanding of what it means to help someone and links it to one of the ways in which Jesus helped the people he met.

■ **Focus for adults:** Jesus was fully human – even to the extent that he had to pay taxes, the same as we do! He understands every detail of our lives, and is more willing to help us than, often, we are to ask.

Touch and talk

Before the start of the session hide a small but important item – eg glasses, one earring, a purse. Near the beginning of the session, express concern that this has gone missing and ask the children to help you look for it. (If this is done well, it appears to be genuine; the glasses are missing just as the leader needs them to read something, the missing earring is suddenly noticed when the leader scratches her ear etc.)

The lost item should not be too obvious, or it will be found inadvertently, nor so well-hidden that it takes too long to find.

Talk about how it feels being helped and helping other people. Do they like being helped? It may be worth pointing out here that genuine help is *wanted*. Small children know only too well the frustration of being helped when they want to do something for themselves!

Talk about ways in which they can help – at home, at playgroup etc. Draw out ways of helping that involve *doing* – like laying the table, helping to put things away; and *not doing* – like not waking the baby when he's asleep, not tipping all the jigsaws out at once and so on. (It's worth noting here that under-fives generally respond better to positive instructions like 'Stay in the house' than to negative ones like 'Don't go outside and get dirty.')

Story presentation

For this simple story use a flannel board or puppets as visual aids, or the story could be dramatised as explained in 'Fish' (page 44).

Peter was out for a walk one day when he was stopped by some important people. They were from the Temple (the Jewish church).

'Excuse us,' they said. 'Everyone has to pay money to the people who look after the Temple. What we want to know is, does your friend Jesus pay it?'

Peter was a bit scared: 'Of course Jesus pays his Temple money,' he said, but he wasn't quite sure. And he'd just remembered that he hadn't paid it, either!

He went home to tell Jesus all about it. 'And what's worse,' he went on, looking a bit glum, 'is that I don't think I've got enough money to pay it.'

'Don't worry,' said Jesus. 'Go to the lake and drop in a fishing-line. Pull up the first fish you catch and look into its mouth.'

Peter did as Jesus told him – and the fish had a silver coin in its mouth! He hurried back to Jesus.

'There you are,' said Jesus, smiling. 'I told you not to worry. Now you can pay the Temple money for both of us!' So, holding the silver coin very tightly, Peter ran off to pay the money.

■ ACTIVITIES
Creative prayer-time

Make a booklet of pictures showing people being helped. Several sheets of coloured sugar paper make a good booklet. Fold them in half and staple them together. Write on the front, 'My Helping Book'. Have a selection of pictures for the children to choose from and help them to stick a picture on each page. Each picture could have a short caption, suggested by the children.

On the first page let the children stick a picture of Jesus helping someone, with the caption, 'Jesus helped.... He will help me, too.'

When everyone has finished, say together, this short responsive prayer:

Lord Jesus,
You helped the lonely people;
Thank you for helping me.
You helped the sick people;
Thank you for helping me.
You helped the sad people;
Thank you for helping me.
And you helped your friends;
Thank you for helping me.

Say at end

Jesus and Peter

Draw a large copy of the picture of Peter and Jesus onto the back of one or two lengths of pre-pasted wall-paper. Have ready lots of different bits of material for clothes, strands of wool for hair, milk bottle tops and coloured foil for the fish and the coin, sand for the ground, dessicated coconut coloured green for the grass, etc, to stick on to the picture. (Wet each part of the picture as you do it, and the materials will stick to it. Have some good PVA glue handy for anything which won't adhere to the paste. Write in large letters underneath the picture: 'Jesus helps his friend Peter.')

A helping game

Play a 'mulberry bush' game based on helping at home. Let the children suggest ways they can help their mums/dads/minders and then use the suggestions in the game:

Here we are, helping at home,
Helping at home, helping at home.
Here we are helping at home,
Helping others for Jesus.

This is the way we… tidy our toys,
  … dust the rooms,
  … brush the floor,
  … do the shopping,
When we're helping at home.

Make a present

Collect yoghurt pots or polystyrene beakers. Let the children decorate them with felt-tip pens, crayons or small cut-out pictures and then fill them with compost. Help them to plant up easily rooted cuttings – tradescantia, spider plants, mother of thousands, etc. Encourage them to give them to someone they know – perhaps an elderly or sick neighbour.

A cheery card

Fold a piece of thin card – about A5 size – in half. Draw a robin on the front. Give a card to each child and let them stick overlapping pieces of red tissue paper on his breast, and brown tissue on his back and wings. His feet and beak may be coloured with crayons or felt tips.

Leaders and other adults can help them write their name and a greeting inside the card.

■ SONGS AND RHYMES

Jesus hands were kind hands CS 45; JP 134
Who does Jesus love? CH 86
* People Jesus helped LJI 68
* Doing the washing FFTB 64

■ The Allabout sheet for this outline is on page 85.

■ POSTMEN & POSTWOMEN

■ **BIBLE LINK: Ephesians 6:21-22 – Tychicus was one of the 'postmen' who delivered the New Testament letters.**
■ **Focus for children:** a simple introduction to the letters of the Bible.
■ **Focus for adults:** the Epistles are a living record of the life of the early church, its practice and beliefs. Many were written to specific groups of people and to deal with particular situations. Members of the churches are often mentioned by name, and sent personal greetings.

Touch and talk

Have a pile of 'post': parcels, letters, birthday cards, postcards etc. Talk about the excitement of post arriving just for *you* – with your name and address on it. You could have some cards in the post for children who have recently had a birthday.

Encourage the children to talk about the post arriving in their home. What time does it arrive? Does the same person bring it each day? How does the postman know it's for you?

Talk about the postman's job. They have a great deal of walking to do, and in all weathers. They are up very early, sometimes in the dark. They get to know lots of people – do they know the children? What happens if a letter isn't properly addressed?

Talk about how to send a letter; how to address the envelope, stamp and post it. What do we post it in? What happens to it then? (Depending on the age of your group you could trace a letter's journey through to the recipient.)

Story presentation

This story is about the way the New Testament letters were written and sent to the Christians in the early church. It is important that there are plenty of bright pictures or OHP slides to give the children a focus.

A long time ago there weren't any church buildings and the people who loved Jesus met together in one

another's homes to talk about him, to pray to him and worship him. The churches were so far away from each other that the people in one church never met the people in another one.

So Paul, one of Jesus' friends, used to write long letters to the people in all the different churches, to encourage them to love Jesus and be his friends.

He wrote his letters on special paper called *parchment*, with a feather made into a pen – called a *quill*.

When he had finished his letter, he sealed it with wax, and made a mark in it to let everyone know it was from him.

Then he sent messengers to take his letters to churches in other countries. These messengers were like postmen for Paul and they had to travel for many weeks to deliver his letters. We know the name of one of his 'postmen'; he was called Tychicus.

The letters that Paul wrote were copied down and kept, and we can

read them in the Bible. They encourage us to love Jesus and be his friends too. (*Show a Bible and point out where the New Testament letters are.*)

• An additional or alternative story can be *Postman Pat Takes a Message* by John Cunliffe (André Deutsch), or *Katie Morag Delivers the Mail* by Mairi Hedderwick (Fontana Picture Lions).

■ ACTIVITIES
Creative prayer-time
• Make a collage-frieze of envelopes and postcards. Collect as many different colours and sizes of envelope as possible and with many different stamps. Use lining paper as a background, and let the children stick on the envelopes and postcards at random.

Across the top of the frieze, write,

'Thank you, God, for the people who bring us letters and parcels.'

Remind them that the people who deliver the post have to get up very early: sing, 'O, Lord! shout for joy!' or 'Get up!'
• Use simple OHP pictures for each line of this prayer:

Thank you, God, for our postman who brings us letters and parcels.
Please keep him safe as he crosses all the roads (or drives his van).
Thank you that there are special letters in the Bible that tell us about you.

Game
The postman's van comes every day (to the tune of 'Here we go round the mulberry bush').

Chorus
The postman's van comes every day,
Every day, every day.
The postman's van comes every day,
Bringing all the post.

The verses go:
This is the way we… write a letter,
  … fold a letter,
  … stamp a letter,
  … post a letter,
Sending love to our friends.

Cards for friends
Make a card for a friend. Have ready a selection of pre-cut pictures, pieces of coloured card and envelopes to fit. Help the children to choose a picture and stick it on to the card. On the back of the card write or help them to write, 'To … with love from ….'

Give each child an envelope and help them put the cards inside. With the help of an adult they can write the name and address on the envelope. If the friend lives nearby, suggest that they 'play postman' themselves and deliver it to the house. (If you have a printing set, the children could put their own 'stamp' on the envelopes, too.)

Post-people
Draw round two or more children lying on large sheets of paper – a boy and a girl. Draw in a postman's/woman's uniform and 'dress' them with pieces of navy-blue material cut to shape. Make milk bottle top buttons and give each one a bulging sack made from brown material suffed with newspaper. You could tuck some old envelopes into the top of their sacks, so that they are just sticking out. Give each of them a hat!

Special delivery!
If there is someone in the group with a birthday coming soon, you could have a 'special delivery'. Choose a child to be postman, give him/her a postman's hat and sack and a sit-and-ride car. Have the 'postman' deliver a birthday card. The group could then sing 'A happy birthday to you' (CSM 36).

■ SONGS AND RHYMES
Writing letters FFTB 65
* Street friends FFTB 84
* I sent a letter to my love TLP 195 or OTU 49
Be kind CS 48 (the words for this song are in one of Paul's letters)
A happy birthday to you CSM 36
O Lord, shout for joy! SSL 4
* Get up! LJI 116

■ The Allabout sheet for this outline is on page 86.

■ DOCTORS, NURSES, HEALTH VISITORS

■ **BIBLE LINK: Mark 2:1-12 – the man let down through the roof.**
■ **Focus for children:** God loves them when they are ill and wants them to be well.
■ **Focus for adults:** God continues his healing work through those involved in medicine and health care, and sometimes intervenes in miraculous ways today, too.

Touch and talk
• Have some scales for the children to weigh themselves and a metre rule (or a tape measure) to measure their height.
• Talk about visits to the well-baby clinic, being weighed and measured, and perhaps seeing the health visitor or nurse. Some of the older children may have had pre-school tests, involving hopping, jumping, skipping, clapping their hands, etc. Ask the children to perform these activities, drawing attention to how well and strong they are.
• Talk about being ill. Did they see the doctor? Who looked after them? Has anyone ever been in hospital, or had a friend or relative in hospital? Some children may be afraid of hospitals, so emphasise that they are good places to be in if someone is sick because everyone there is helping them to get better. Remind them that parents are allowed to stay with children, that there are lots of toys to play with and that everyone is very kind. If you can, invite a doctor or nurse to the group, preferably with their 'working clothes' on, and involve them at this stage.

Story presentation
For this story you will need four strips of card, about 3 cm by 15 cm, joined end to end with a butterfly fastener. During the story you will use the strip to make: pictures of a figure **4**, a **bed**, a **door**, a **house** (with a **flat roof** or a **pointed roof**), **stairs** and a **hole**.

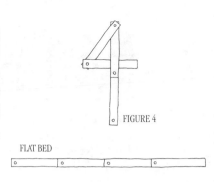

FIGURE 4

FLAT BED

BED WITH LEGS / DOOR / HOUSE (FLAT ROOF)

HOUSE (POINTED ROOF)

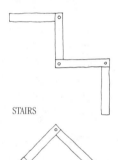

STAIRS

A HOLE

In the country where Jesus lived there were no nurses, no hospitals and very few doctors. People who were ill were looked after by their friends and family. Today we're going to hear a story about one man whose friends were very kind to him and helped him to get better.

Once there was a very sick man who had to stay in bed all the time. (Let's call him Abel.) His **bed** was flat on the floor like this, not like your **beds** at home. Abel had **four** friends who came to see him every day and looked after him.

They were worried about Abel because he was so ill and couldn't get up. They wanted to take him to Jesus because they knew he could make their friend well again.

So one day the four friends carried Abel on his **bed** to the house where Jesus was.

But when they got to the **house** where Jesus was, it was so full of people, they couldn't get in through the **door**.

Houses in Jesus country didn't have roofs like ours – **pointed** – they were **flat** and they had the **stairs** on the outside.

So the **four** friends carried Abel up the **stairs** on to the **flat roof** (it was **flat** not **pointed**) and **laid** him down carefully. They looked at each other.

'What can we do?' asked one. 'We can't get Abel in through the **door**. We can't get Abel in through the window. We'll have to get him in through the **roof**.'

So they began to make a **hole** in the **roof**! When it was big enough, they said to Abel, 'Don't worry. You'll soon be seeing Jesus. Hold on tightly!'

They let Abel down, still on his **bed**, very, very carefully. Jesus was surprised to see Abel comong down towards him, and so was everyone else!

Jesus made Abel better at once. 'Get up!' he said. '**Fold up** your bed and go home.' And Abel found that he could. He stood up and walked, carrying his **bed**. His friends were very glad that they'd taken Abel to see Jesus.

■ ACTIVITIES
Creative prayer-time

Make a prayer book about the people who help us when we're ill. Collect pictures of any aspect of nursing and hospital care (avoiding, if possible, a 'doctors are men, nurses are women' stereotype). Include some pictures of mummies, daddies or grandparents helping small children when they are ill.

Give each child a booklet made from coloured sugar paper and help them to stick a picture on each page of their book. If they are able they may like to write a simple prayer on each page (eg, 'Thank you God for nurses'). Write on the front of the booklet something like: 'Thank you God for the people who help us when we are ill,' or, 'Please help all the people who take care of us.'

'Being well' frieze

Make a frieze of healthy children involved in all sorts of activities. Include, if possible, drawings or pictures of children at the well-baby clinic. Give it a simple heading like: 'Thank you God that you want us to be well.'

Talk about how God wants us to keep healthy (by eating good food, putting on coats to go outside in cold weather etc).

Doctors and nurses game

Make up a bag of items a doctor or nurse might use: thermometer, stethoscope, spatula, bandage, tweezers, scissors, pen, watch, syringe, cream, plasters....

Let the children take out one item in turn and try to guess what it is used for.

Make a display of all the items on a small table.

Ambulance montage

Draw a large outline of an ambulance on a piece of lining paper or newsprint. Let the children stick on pieces of scrunched-up tissue paper: white for the main body, blue for the light on top, black for the wheels and perhaps a red cross on the side.

Talk to the children all about ambulances as you do it.

A picture to take home

Give each child a pre-drawn picture of Jesus healing the paralysed man and let them enjoy colouring it in with felt tips or crayons.

■ SONGS AND RHYMES

Jesus loves Kristi FS 83
* I have hands that will clap, clap, clap CSM 25
* Jump for Jesus CSM 2
* Miss Polly had a dolly OTU 17
* People Jesus helped LJI 68
* Lord, You put some bounce in my feet IFW 58

■ The Allabout sheet for this outline is on page 86.

Theme rhymes for the 'Weather' series:
'Thank you for the world you made' LJI 13
'Seasons song' LJI 20.

■ SUN

■ **BIBLE LINK: Genesis 1:14-19.**
■ **Background:** in temperate zones people welcome the sun and feel they don't get enough of it, but in hotter climates people are more concerned to shelter from it; so references to the sun in the Bible often view it as a danger rather than a blessing. We can still stress to the children how much we and all living things need the sun's light and warmth.
■ **Focus for children:** God is in charge of the weather; let's be thankful for the sun and warm weather.
■ **Focus for adults:** in Psalm 84:11 God is described as 'a sun' – the source of spiritual light and warmth. In Malachi 4:2 the prophet describes the coming of Jesus as like the sun rising, the rays of the sun bringing healing and hope.

Touch and talk
Bring in a selection of items or pictures we associate with warm weather – sunglasses, buckets and spades, swimsuits, suncream, beach towels, and perhaps pictures of garden furniture, barbecues, deck-chairs and tropical beaches.

Ask the children to tell you what sort of weather/days the things you've brought are for, and establish that they're all for warm sunny days. Ask if any children have been to the seaside on a hot day etc.

Story presentation
Emphasise that God made the sun and the moon and stars a long long time ago, to give us light by day and by night. A dull day, when the clouds hide the sun, is much darker than a day when the sun is shining brightly. The sun also keeps us warm, and helps plants to grow.

■ ACTIVITIES
Creative prayer-time/visual display
Cut a large circle out of yellow paper or card and write on it, 'God made the sun'. Give each child a 'ray' of the sun to colour red, yellow or gold, and write their names on if they can. (If you have time you could let them do the rays of the sun with montage – small bits of coloured paper or scrunched-up tissues or tissue paper stuck on.) Attach all the rays to the sun, and thank God for its light and warmth, perhaps using the action rhyme 'The sun'.

Flower pictures
Give each child a piece of paper bearing the words 'The sun helps the flowers grow'. Let them colour the top half blue and the bottom half green. Give them a yellow circle for the sun to be stuck at the top, and then let them cut out or choose pictures of flowers from gardening catalogues, to stick on the green part.

Ice-cream cornets
Cut out cornet shapes (long narrow triangles) in a neutral coloured paper and circles to represent ice-cream and let the children stick them together on a sheet of paper. They could stick on cotton wool balls (white or coloured) to give a 3-D effect to the ice-cream.

Sun masks
Cut circles of stiff yellow paper or thin card, allowing two or three inches around the edge to make the sun's rays. Cut the rays of the sun, and two holes for eyes, and let children draw on a face, colour in the rays, or stick gold and silver glitter on. Fasten the masks with shirring elastic.

■ SONGS AND RHYMES
The sun LJI 14
* Incey wincey spider RRG 17
The sun has got his hat on (traditional)
* Your shadow FFTB 29
I love the sun SSL 12
We praise you for the sun SSL 13
And see the list at the top of this page.

■ The Allabout sheet for this outline is on page 87.

■ COLD WEATHER

■ **BIBLE LINK: Psalm 147:16-17 or Proverbs 31:13,19,21.**
■ **Background:** there are no 'stories' as such in the Bible about snow, since it rarely ocurred, though some mountains were high enough to be snowcapped. However there are numerous references to snow, and to the fact that it is part of God's creation, as the verses from Psalm 147 show. These are a little abstract for under-fives so we suggest you either just refer to them briefly and stress that God makes and sends snow or use the Proverbs passage, making it into a narrative.
■ **Focus for children:** God rules the weather; let's thank him for different aspects of cold weather.
■ **Focus for adults:** in western culture housewives and mothers are continually downgraded and it's interesting that in Bible times, when women didn't count for much, the Proverbs passage is full of praise for someone who was not just housewife, but also businesswoman.

Touch and talk
• Dress up in warm coat/anorak, scarf, hat, gloves and thick socks and boots, and ask the children what sort of weather you're dressed for. Talk about their replies, being sure to keep within their experience, both actual and via books and TV. If you live in an area where you regularly get snow and ice, you will probably find the children will talk about sledging and making snowmen as things they have actually done, whereas some children will never have experienced snow. Talk about frost and icicles – show a picture if possible. All children have some understanding of the difference between cold and warm weather and the unit is called 'cold weather' so that you can adapt it appropriately.
• Have a selection of pictures for them to look at and talk about. Pictures of Eskimos, igloos and polar bears, or of skiers would make a change from more usual cold weather scenes and probably stimulate questions. If you have no big pictures, Christmas cards often have scenes with snow, snowmen, skaters,

frost and ice, and children can handle these easily.

• Most children are absolutely fascinated by 'snowstorm' novelties – a liquid-filled glass or plastic globe with figures or landscape, which when shaken has an effect of falling snow. Try to borrow several of these as everyone will want a turn.

Story presentation
• **Psalm 147**

Start by mentioning an activity or song about cold weather that you have already enjoyed. Ask who makes the cold weather and the snow. Then say 'One of the songs in God's book, the Bible, talks about snow; this is what it says: (read from the Good News Bible).'

• or **Proverbs 31**

When it's cold here, what sort of clothes do we need? Warm ones, that's right. Where do we get them? Usually we buy them in a shop. Sometimes mums or grannies or aunties knit them for us. Where do they get the wool? From a shop.

In Bible times, it didn't snow very often, but they had cold weather, especially at night, so people needed warm clothes. But they didn't buy them from a shop; they had to make them. If they wanted wool, they couldn't just go and buy some balls of wool; they had to buy a sheep's woolly coat from a shepherd, take it home and wash it and comb it, and spin it with a spinning wheel. Then they could use the thread to make warm clothes.

One lady did that in the Bible; we don't know her name so let's call her Anna. She was always busy, looking after her house and her children, shopping and cooking, buying and selling. She bought wool from the shepherd and made it into thread. Then she dyed it lovely colours, and made thick warm clothes for her husband and her children. She wasn't afraid of snowy weather; even if it was very cold she knew her family would be all right because she had worked so hard to make them nice warm clothes.

■ ACTIVITIES
Creative prayer-time/visual display

(This activity is suitable for children who can manage scissors – probably four year olds. Children who can't

manage scissors could possibly tear theirs or be given some snowflakes to put glitter or salt on.)

Give each child one or more circles of white paper, about the size of a teaplate, folded as shown. Let them cut or tear pieces out of the three edges of the paper so that when they open it out a 'snowflake' appears, which can be further decorated by the addition of glitter – or salt. Children like the end product of this activity, but may find it difficult to cut or tear several layers of paper, so have plenty of snowflakes ready-made for children to add salt or glitter to, but also have several white paper circles available for children who are desperate to have a go – perhaps assisted by an adult. Stand with the children in a circle and let them all hold up a snowflake while you thank God briefly for the fun and beauty of snow. Mount some of the snowflakes on black or dark blue paper headed, 'God sends the snow'.

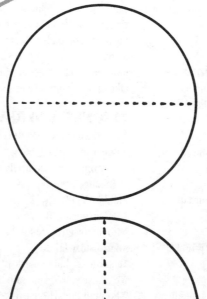

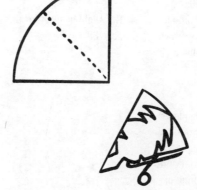

Snowman
Give each child a piece of paper with a simple snowman outline. Let them glue on cotton wool for his body, and buttons, sequins, currants or black sticky circles for buttons or eyes. Add a scrap of colourful material or paper for a scarf, and provide some cut-out hat shapes in a contrasting colour. Let the children draw in a mouth and nose.

Paper snowmen
The paper dollies activity in 'Friends' (page 46) can be adapted for paper snowmen.

Cutting and sticking
Let children cut or choose winter scenes from old Christmas cards and stick them on to a large sheet of paper.

Fire collage/painting
Point out that when it's cold we like to have warm houses. Some people have radiators or gas fires, but some people have fires of logs and coal. Draw a simple outline of flames and let the children stick on scraps of material or paper in red, orange and yellow. At the top of the paper write, 'Fires keep us warm in cold weather'. Alternatively let children paint fires – red, yellow and orange paint is particularly effective on black paper.

Warm up
Ask children to pretend it's a cold day; what do they do? Why? (Demonstrate shivering and use the word several times if it seems unfamiliar.) Say that if we're cold we can warm up by doing exercises, and take the group through some simple but vigorous ones – to music if you have a suitable tape.

■ SONGS AND RHYMES
* This is how the snowflakes play about TLP 59
* Little snowman FFTB 34
Polar bear FFTB 36
* Icicles FFTB 44
* Skiing FFTB 170
The North wind doth blow (traditional)
* Here we go round the mulberry bush on a cold and frosty morning (traditional)
And see the list on page 54.

■ The Allabout sheet for this outline is on page 87.

■ RAIN

■ **BIBLE LINK: Noah – Genesis 7-8 and 9:8-17.**

■ **Focus for children:** God sends and controls the rain. We need it.

■ **Focus for adults:** God keeps his promises – every time we see a rainbow we can be reminded of that.

Touch and talk

Dress up in wellingtons, mac and rain hat and carry the largest umbrella you can find (borrow a fisherman's or golfing umbrella if possible). Ask the children if they can guess why you're dressed like that, and talk to them about rain in general.

Story presentation

There are many beautifully illustrated books about Noah for young children; you could use the pictures from one as you tell the story, or make a simple ark from a shoe box, adding a sloping roof, and using zoo animals.

■ ACTIVITIES
Creative prayer-time

Make a circle and sing to the tune of 'Here we go round the mulberry bush', with appropriate actions.

This is the way the rain comes down,
rain comes down,
rain comes down,
This is the way the rain comes down –
Thank you, God, for rain!

This is the way the flowers grow…
When God sends the rain!

This is the way we splash in puddles…
Thank you, God, for rain!

Visual display

Let each child colour an umbrella shape, which can then be stuck onto a large sheet of paper and handles drawn in. Add some large clear-cellophane raindrops.

Montage wellingtons

Give each child a piece of strong paper on which is drawn a large clear outline of a pair of wellingtons. Provide pieces of torn up paper in a bright colour and let them stick them onto the outline of the wellingtons. (They will need help with this; suggest they put glue on the large sheet of paper not on the torn up squares.) As a finishing touch you could add 'puddles' of shiny black paper.

Frogs

Explain that frogs like rain too! Give each child the basic shape cut from a folded piece of paper (see pattern) and green crayons (unless you have cut the shapes from green paper or card). Next add eyes (large white circles with black dots) and finally fold back a little of the front edge to make a mouth, and add a tongue in felt-tip pen. If time allows let children make more than one frog in different sizes so that they have a frog family.

Rainbows

Give each child a sheet of paper with a sun in the top left hand corner and a cloud with rain coming from it in the top right hand corner, and a rainbow shape in the centre. At the bottom write, 'The sun and the rain together make a rainbow'. Let the children colour in the rainbow or, if you have enough help, let them stick on balls of scrunched-up coloured tissue paper. The montage looks more effective but will probably take most of your activity time.

■ SONGS AND RHYMES

* Incey-wincey spider RRG 17
* I hear thunder TLP 60
* Pray open your umbrella TLP 62
    (change pray to please)
Rainbows FFTB 26
* Raindrops FFTB 32
* Noah noise rhyme LJI 24
Noah's story LJI 26
Mister Noah built an ark JP 167
We praise you for the rain SSL 13
Who built the ark? SSL 44
Sing a rainbow – Apusskidu (see page 15 for details)
And see the list on page 54.

■ The Allabout sheet for this outline is on page 88.

WIND AND AIR

■ **BIBLE LINK: Luke 8:22-25 – Jesus calms the storm.**
■ **Focus for children:** God controls the wind and gives us the air we breathe.
■ **Focus for adults:** despite the disciples' fears, Jesus was in control even of the storm. He asked why they didn't trust him. He wants us to trust him even when life is 'stormy'.

Touch and talk

Have ready one or more of the following for children to look at, handle and talk about: a plastic toy or model windmill of the kind sold in garden centres, some blown up balloons (or keep these hidden till prayer-time – see below), a set of windchimes, a tub of bubble mixture. Blow bubbles, or blow on the windmill and windchimes. Explain simply that though we can't see it, there is air all around us. When the air is moving we call it wind or a breeze. Balloons are full of air, so are the bubbles. When we breathe we take air into our bodies. Let them put their hands on their chests and breathe deeply in and out so that they can feel their lungs inflating and deflating – 'going up and down'.

Story presentation

Introduce the story by saying that very strong winds make big waves on the sea; we call that a storm. You may wish to add drama by having a blue blanket on the floor (which adults can ripple) to represent the sea, and having the children sit in cardbord box 'boats'.

■ ACTIVITIES
Creative prayer-time

Before everyone arrives, blow up lots of balloons, perhaps leaving one to inflate in the children's presence as a visual aid. Add strings to the balloons so that children can hold them easily, stand in a circle and remind them that the balloons are full of air. Wave your balloons and sing a praise song that the children know well, then throw all your balloons into the air and try to catch them again. (Have some spares in case of accidents!)

Bubble pictures

Half fill three or four small containers (eg margarine cartons) with warm water to which you have added paint or food colouring and a little washing up liquid. Put a straw in each bowl. Children or helpers blow gently into the water till the bubbles rise above the rim, then carefully place a sheet of white paper over the top. The bubble pattern will transfer to the paper and the process can be repeated with the next colour. Give each child his/her own straw and make sure they blow and don't suck! (It's a good idea to have a trial run with this one to get proportions right.) If each child does two or more, you could display one from each child all together on a contrasting sheet of paper for a visual display. Grouping them together is very effective, and you could head the display, 'We made these pictures with bubbles full of air'.

Painting: blob and blow

Drop a blob of fairly runny paint onto a piece of paper and blow gently through a straw to get a shape; fold this over to get a symmetrical shape. (Again – don't let children suck!)

■ SONGS AND RHYMES
* Clouds FFTB 28
* A windy day FFTB 30
* Falling fir trees FFTB 125
* The feather FFTB 131
* Blowing bubbles FFTB 164
* My little house won't stand up straight TLP 28
* Five little leaves so bright and gay TLP 89
* Jesus calms the storm

Jesus is in his friends' fishing boat,
Don't wake him – he's fast asleep;
    (*head on hands*)
His friends are rowing across the lake,
    (*mime rowing*)
The water is cold and deep. (*shiver*)

But look! The wind is starting to blow,
    (*wind noises!*)
The water's getting rough! (*show waves with hands*)
The men are rowing very hard (*speed up rowing action*)
But can't go fast enough. (*shake head*)

The wind is blowing loud and strong,
    (*cup ear with hand*)
The waves are getting high, (*indicate height*)
Jesus' friends are really scared, (*look frightened*)
They think they're going to die!

'Wake up, Jesus!' somebody says,
    (*mime shaking awake*)
'HE will know what to do;'
Jesus wakes up, looks round and says,
    (*look all round*)
'Don't worry any of you.'

He speaks to the wind and the frightening waves,
And tells them to go away;
At once the wind and the waves calm down –
It's Jesus they must obey.

And see the list on page 54.

■ The Allabout sheet for this outline is on page 88.

CHRISTMAS

The five visual displays in the four units in this series are intended to build up into one large display telling the Christmas story from the annunciation to the wise men.

It is difficult to find really original activities suitable for under-fives at Christmas, but we need to remember that things which seem 'old hat' to us are all new and exciting when you're three or four years old.

CHRISTMAS 1
■ THE ANNUNCIATION

■ **BIBLE LINK: Luke 1:26-38.**
■ **Background:** although traditionally angels (God's messengers) are depicted as white shining beings with wings, they seem to have appeared often in the form of ordinary human beings. However it's probably simpler at this stage to represent them traditionally, to avoid confusion in young minds.
■ **Focus for children:** a message for Mary.
■ **Focus for adults:** Mary didn't understand, but she trusted and accepted God's word.

Touch and talk
Bring in some messages – letters, postcards, a telephone (real or toy), birthday and Christmas cards, wedding and party invitations, and a birth announcement card, even the 'Personal column' of the local paper. If you have only a small group you could write a card for each child with a brief message like, 'We would like to see you at…' and the name of your group, or an invitation to the group's Christmas party. Put the cards in envelopes and address them to individual children. Talk about the other 'messages' first, asking the children if they know what sort of messages they are: holiday postcards, birth announcements and party invitations/birthday cards can often be recognised even by children who can't yet read. Then give the children their own envelopes, or ask if they have ever taken a message – have they ever gone and asked Granny if she wants a cup of tea, or told Daddy that dinner is ready? Today's story is about a very important message – from God!

Story presentation
You could act out the story simply, with one leader as Mary and another as the angel, or make two simple puppets,

perhaps from wooden spoons or paper bags.

■ ACTIVITIES
Creative prayer-time
Sing 'Oh Mary's busy sweeping' to the tune 'Poor Jenny sits a-weeping' (traditional). Move round in a circle, miming appropriate actions:

Oh Mary's busy sweeping, sweeping, sweeping,
Oh Mary's busy sweeping, at home in Nazareth.
(*Mime sweeping*)

Now Mary sees an angel, an angel with a message,
She listens to the message, the message from God.
(*Throw up hands in surprise, then cup ear as if listening*)

You're going to have a baby, a baby called Jesus,
You're going to have a baby – he'll be God's own Son.
(*Look pleased, rock baby in arms*)

Oh thank you, God, for Jesus, for Jesus, for Jesus,
Oh thank you, God, for Jesus, your own special Son!
(*Skip in circle and clap hands*)

Visual display – section 1
On a large sheet of paper outline the figures of Mary, perhaps sweeping, and the angel, against a simple background of a house interior. If you want extra detail, you could put in some palm trees or a few extra figures outside. Let the children help make a collage of the scene. If you prefer, you could collage individual figures, pieces of furniture etc, and mount them on to a backing sheet later.

Message cards
Give each child a piece of folded card, and let them choose from a selection of coloured heart shapes, explaining that we use the heart to send the message, 'I love you'. If you want to be Christmassy, cut heart shapes out of Christmas wrapping paper; if you feel it's too early for that, cut them out of coloured paper, or shiny gummed paper. Let the children stick the hearts onto the front of the card, and decorate with glitter or with crayons, or anything else suitable. Inside, write 'I love you' and ask each child whose name they would like added.

Heart biscuits
Use any simple biscuit recipe, and cut out heart-shaped biscuits. Let the children decorate them with glace icing, and 'sprinkles' (silver balls, tiny pieces of chopped up glace cherries etc). Make clear to them before you start that these are a special 'message' for them to take to someone to say, 'I love you'.

Angels
• **Paper angels** See the instructions for paper dollies in the 'Friends' outline (page 46) and adapt to form paper angels. Few children will be able to cut angels out for themselves, but if you can cut them out beforehand children would enjoy decorating them with glitter or crayons.

• **Angel stencils** Provide some simple angel stencils cut out of polythene ice-cream carton lids. Use Blu-tack to stick stencils to paper while the children colour them in.

• **Angel templates** Use stiff card to make several angel templates for children to draw round (or provide ready-drawn outlines). As with stencils, anchor the template to the paper with Blu-tack as small children find it difficult to hold the template steady and draw round it. Let them decorate angels with sequins, glitter, milk bottle tops, even scraps of tinsel, or pieces of lacy paper doilies.

• **Polystyrene angels!** Polystyrene cups are very stable if you wanted to make, say, a crib scene or a model of the angels appearing to the shepherds. (If you can't get hold of them, yoghurt pots would do, but you would then need to cover them with gold or silver paper to hide the lettering.) In addition you will need white paper tissues, cheap white net – the sort soap is wrapped in to sell at school fairs! – or old nylon tights – the paler the better – and white, gold or silver card or stiff paper and/or paper doilies. Make a ball of two or three white tissues, and put it into a square of netting or old tights, tying it at the bottom leaving a longish end. With a knitting needle, carefully make a hole in the bottom of the inverted polystyrene cup, and push the ends of the net/tights through to give the angel's head. Wings are made from a semicircle of paper/card. Attach the wings to the cup with sticky tape behind the head. This gives a very basic angel but you could vary many details: the edge of the wings for example could be cut into a decorative pattern with pinking shears, or a folded doiley could be used; you could use contrasting material for the wings, add glitter or sequins, cover the cup itself with net, and add a piece of tinsel to the angel's head…

■ SONGS AND RHYMES

Mary's surprise LJI 49
The angel one day CS 22
God's angel came to Mary CS 23

■ The Allabout sheet for this outline is on page 89.

CHRISTMAS 2
■ THE JOURNEY TO BETHLEHEM

■ **BIBLE LINK:** Luke 2:1-7.
■ **Background:** Nazareth was about 70 miles from Bethlehem, a long journey for a pregnant woman. She probably travelled at least part of the way by donkey, though the Bible gives no details.
■ **Focus for children:** preparations for the special baby, the journey to Bethlehem and Jesus' birth.
■ **Focus for adults:** no room in the inn – so often, in all the preparations for Christmas, we too have no room for Christ.

Touch and talk

Bring in clothes and equipment for a newborn baby for the children to handle and talk about – stress how tiny the things are and how important it is for babies to be kept warm and clean and fed, as they can do nothing for themselves.

Story presentation

Remind children of the angel's message to Mary, and stress preparations for the new baby – clothes and maybe a wooden cradle made by Joseph, Mary's husband, who was a carpenter; the long journey to Bethlehem, on foot or by donkey; no room when they reach there – everywhere full; Jesus born in a stable, and a manger for his cradle.

■ ACTIVITIES
Creative prayer-time

If possible, 'borrow' a young baby from someone in the group, or use a large doll. Put the baby (or the doll) in a box with straw as the manger in the centre, and group the children around. Sing a short, familiar Christmas song, such as 'Away in a manger' before thanking God very simply and briefly for all babies, and especially for sending baby Jesus.

Visual display – sections 2 and 3

This week's display is probably most easily done in two halves, the first showing Mary and Joseph travelling towards Bethlehem (children could collage figures of Mary, Joseph and donkey, and stick houses and trees on for Bethlehem), the second showing a stable scene with the manger and the baby – perhaps with real straw on the floor and in the manger.

Stable pictures

This activity needs advance preparation, which will be simplifed if you have access to a photocopier, but is not impossible without. Children like matching shapes, so make simple templates of Mary and Joseph, the manger, and perhaps one or two animals – a cow and a donkey. Make sure they will all fit on the size of paper you'll use! Draw round the templates so that the outlines are on the sheets, and then from stiff paper or card cut out enough shapes for every child to have one of each. Help the children match the shapes with the outlines on the paper and stick them on. If there is time the pictures could then be coloured, or you could cut each outline from a different coloured paper – a grey donkey, brown cow, black manger, blue Mary, red Joseph.

Birth announcements

Explain that often parents send cards to their friends telling them a new baby has arrived, and you are going to do that for Jesus. Give each child a piece of paper with the words 'Baby Jesus is here' and let them stick on pictures of babies cut from old mail order, Boots or Mothercare catalogues, or decorate with gummed paper shapes.

Donkey puppets

On stiff paper, or preferably card, outline the head and neck of a donkey. These can then be inserted into houseplant canes. Once the basic outline is done, the puppet can be as simple or elaborate as you have time for – children could draw in eyes and ears, or they could be cut from paper and stuck on, and the donkey's mane could be made from grey or brown crepe paper and glued on. Children would enjoy holding these puppets to sing 'Little Donkey'.

■ SONGS AND RHYMES
Away in a manger
Little Donkey CGC 3
Mary had a baby, yes Lord CP2 123
Sweet Mary LJI 54
Baby born in Bethlehem CSM 45

■ The Allabout sheet for this outline is on page 89.

■ THE SHEPHERDS 1993?

■ **BIBLE LINK: Luke 2:8-20.**
■ **Focus for children:** God sent angels to tell shepherds about the very special baby.
■ **Focus for adults:** the shepherds' response to the message was eager and immediate; is ours?

Touch and talk
Let the children handle clothes made of wool, a ball of knitting wool, a woollen travel-rug, some sheep's wool, or slippers or mittens. Do they know where all these things come from? Talk about sheep, showing pictures of sheep and lambs. Ask what we call the man who looks after sheep, to ensure that the children are familiar with the word 'shepherd' – otherwise today's story is meaningless!

Story presentation
This is suitable for the storyteller to dress up in Middle Eastern style clothes for a semi-dramatic telling of the story.

■ ACTIVITIES
Creative prayer-time/drama activity
Teach children the first verse of 'Sing a song of Christmas' to the tune of 'Sing a song of sixpence', (LJI 48), and then thank God simply for sending Jesus. If you have only a small group you could dress them all up as shepherds (remind adults the previous week to bring in dressing-gowns, towels or tea towels, and the stretchy band cut from the top of a pair of nylon tights) and mime the story (after the original telling) to a leader's narration before singing the song in costume.

Sing a song of Christmas, a baby in the hay,
Sing a song for Jesus, born on Christmas day.
Sing a song of shepherds; angels said to them,
'Go and see the baby who is born in Bethlehem.'

Visual display – section 4
Add figures of shepherds and sheep and perhaps a collage fire, with a chorus of angels in the sky. This section lends itself particularly well to being done by a large group, as each child could do an angel or a sheep, or one of each, with adults doing the shepherds. Sheep could have coats of cotton wool; angels could be decorated as in 'Christmas 1'.

• **Shepherds** Outline a simple figure of a shepherd, perhaps holding a sheep, or with one at his feet. Let the children colour the picture or stick on pieces of cloth for his clothes, and maybe a twig for his crook, and put cotton wool on the sheep.

• **Angels** Use any of the angel activities described in the outline for 'Christmas 1' but not used then.

• **Pipe cleaner sheep** Twist three pipe cleaners into a basic sheep shape for each child, using one for the head, back and tail, and one each for two pairs of legs. Let children wind oddments of white, grey, beige/cream or black wool round the bodies – if you can find chunky or textured wool so much the better. These sheep should stand up.

■ SONGS AND RHYMES
Baa baa black sheep (traditional)
Sing a song of Christmas LJI 48 – first verse
Sweet Mary LJI 54

■ The Allabout sheet for this outline is on page 90.

CHRISTMAS 4
■ THE WISE MEN

■ CHRISTINGLE SERVICE

This has been planned as the climax of an Advent programme. If you want to use this as a 'one-off' service, you may need to change the Bible story so that you include the story of Jesus' birth. Some groups may feel that they want to keep the story of the wise men until Epiphany, but beware of using the story of the wise men so long after Christmas that the children have forgotten the other Christmas stories. As the story tells of the wise men bringing presents to Jesus this unit could, if you felt it appropriate, be used as a 'toy service' where children bring gifts for those in need.

The Christingle has become very popular in Britain in recent years. The word Christingle means 'Christ-light' and the Christingle is a wonderful visual symbol of the whole Christian message: the orange represents the world; the candle stands for Jesus, the light of the world; the red ribbon the blood of Christ shed for the sins of the world; the four sticks remind us that God's children will be gathered from east and west, north and south; while the fruits and nuts remind us of God's abundant goodness and provision. In our family we each have a lighted Christingle on the breakfast table every Christmas morning; after all the excitement of stocking-opening it reminds us again of what Christmas is really about.

• **To make a Christingle** you will need: an orange, a small red, green or white candle, about 10-14 cm long, four wooden cocktail sticks, thin red ribbon (or red sticky tape or even red tinsel), dried fruit or glace cherries and monkey nuts in their shells, plus a little aluminium foil (to line the candle hole), a few pins (to secure the ribbon) and an apple corer (to make the candle hole). Assemble the various bits as shown in the diagram on this page.

It will be obvious that a child under five cannot really make a Christingle, even with adult help, so if you plan to hold a Christingle service, you need to decide well in advance who will make the Christingles and when.

■ **BIBLE LINK: Matthew 2:1-12.**
■ **Background:** the 'wise men' of the biblical story have come to be called kings. They probably came from Persia (now Iran) and because three gifts are mentioned we have come to assume there were three of them, though Matthew does not actually say this! It is probable that the wise men visited much later than the shepherds. However, these points are probably too confusing for children who will see numerous pictures of kings worshipping with the shepherds, so omit them.
■ **Focus for children:** wise men followed the star to find Jesus.
■ **Focus for adults:** the wise men followed a star – to find Jesus, the light of the world.

Touch and talk

Display a variety of lights – a torch, Christmas tree lights, candles of different shapes and sizes, a hurricane lamp or a 'camping Gaz' lantern, any other kind of light you can find and, of course, the Christingle. Let children look at these and talk about them.

Remind everyone that all these lights need something else to make them work – a torch needs a battery, a lamp needs to be plugged in and switched on, a candle has to be lit, and a paraffin lamp has to have enough fuel to burn to make a light. Then show pictures of the sun, moon and stars: these are God's lights, and they don't need batteries or electricity – they just keep shining! The last part of our Christmas story today is about one of God's lights – a very special star.

Story presentation

It's probably simpler with this age-group to omit Herod's deception and the warning of the dream; concentrate on

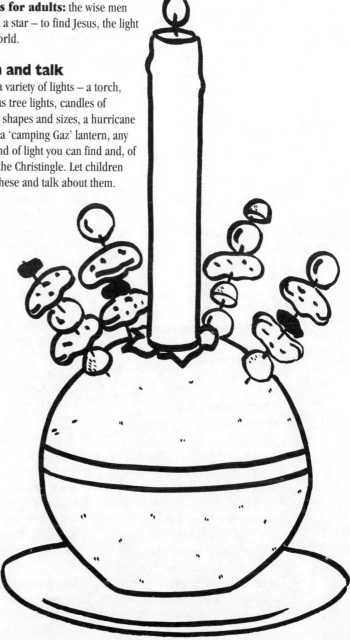

the bare essentials – the wise men saw the star, they went to the palace because they thought that's where the baby king would be, but were directed to Bethlehem, where the star guided them to Jesus; they gave him lovely special presents. (Have a large star and three interestingly shaped and gift-wrapped parcels for the appropriate points in the story.) Children may not be familiar with the meaning of the word 'wise', so explain that it means very clever.

■ ACTIVITIES
Creative prayer-time

Remind children that many people were happy and excited when Jesus was born. God wants us to be happy too. Teach children the second verse of 'Sing a song of Christmas' – see below (LJI 48). Display the words for adults to join in, and either let the children hold the stars they have made as they stand in a circle to sing (see activity below), or have in the centre the star and wrapped gifts used as visual aids for the story.

① Sing a song of wise men following the star,

② Bringing gifts to Jesus, travelling oh so far.

③ Sing a song for Jesus, lying in the hay,

Born to make us happy, born for us on Christmas day! → *see over*

④

Alternatively you could use 'Babies' (LJI 55) as a shared prayer today.

Visual display – section 5

Add to the display today one large star and lots of small ones (maybe gummed paper stars), the wise men, in shiny robes and perhaps on camels, and the gifts they brought.

Christmas tree star

You need card, pasta shapes, hole-punch, glue, ribbon, spray-paint, newspaper to protect furniture, and glitter. Cut fairly large, simple star shapes out of thin card, punching a small hole in the top of each, and let the children glue on pasta shapes; spray with gold or silver paint (not in the same room as the children) and let the children add glitter. Attach a ribbon or metallic thread through the hole. Put children's names or initials on the back before starting, as they all look very

similar. (These make very effective tree decorations and last for years.)

Christmas candles

You need small pots, small candles, plaster of Paris and some trimming – ribbon, tinsel, tape etc. Have ready for each child a small 'fromage frais' pot, or a small washing-liquid lid, in green, red or white. Mix up some plaster of Paris and put enough in each pot for a small candle to stay upright. Let the children put in the candles and help them tie a piece of coloured ribbon or tinsel round the base of each candle. (Alternatively they could decorate the pots with sticky stars or Christmas tape before putting in the candles.) They now have a present to give to someone special at Christmas.

Stained glass windows

You need black paper or card and coloured tissue paper in yellow and one other colour, perhaps green or red.

From the card cut out a stencil-type candle shape in two parts, ie the flame and the body of the candle. On the wrong side of the card write the child's name or initials, and then let them stick a square of yellow tissue paper over the flame hole and a rectangle of coloured tissue paper over the candle hole. Turn back to the right side and use a 'glue pen' to make rays coming from the candle flame; the children can sprinkle these with glitter. The candle can be stuck on a window where the light shining through will give the effect of stained glass.

■ SONGS AND RHYMES

As you sing today, it would add to the atmosphere if Christingles or candles could be lit; work out beforehand exactly how you will do this safely. Use songs which the children know already, and which you have been singing in the last few weeks. Songs especially appropriate today include:

Sing a song of Christmas LJI 48
Wise men's surprise LJI 52
Great wise men LJI 53
Follow the light LJI 53
Twinkle twinkle little star (traditional)

After the service you could serve refreshments – make them festive! Use gold and silver doileys and Christmas

napkins; serve biscuits in the shape of stars for the children, and mince pies with pastry stars for parents and visitors.

Today encourage people to come to church at Christmas. You could have a display of Christmas books for adults and children! Consider giving each child a card and an inexpensive gift-wrapped Christian book.

■ The Allabout sheet for this outline is on page 90.

③ Sing a song of Jesus
a very special boy
sent by God to all
of us to spread the
christmas joy.

④

The following Festival Services outlines have been written with a wider age range in mind than the rest of the outlines in this book. We have assumed that some churches may want to use these Festival outlines for all-age services which have an emphasis on younger children's needs. However, they would be equally suitable for a special service for parents and under-fives.

■ CAROL SERVICE

■ **BIBLE LINK: Luke 2:1-20 and Hebrews 1:1-6.**

■ **Focus for children:** the real meaning of Christmas and why we give gifts. The 'best' presents are when we give something of ourselves, and God gave the best present of all when he sent his Son into the world.

■ **Focus for adults and older children:** God's greatest gift to us is his Son, Jesus. He made it possible for us to be God's friends.

■ OUTLINE
Carol
Girls and boys, leave your toys CGC 12

Touch and talk
Have about five Christmas presents, beautifully wrapped and looking very exciting and mysterious, in a prominent place. How do the children feel, seeing the presents? Can they guess what's inside them? If they could choose one, which would it be? Are there exciting-looking presents at home?

Talk about their own Christmas preparations. Who do they give presents to? Do they make or buy them? Have they finished wrapping up their presents yet? What have they done with them – hidden them or put them by the tree?

Singing game
Sing 'Jesus was born on Christmas Day' (to the tune 'Here we go round the mulberry bush').

Chorus
(children join hands and walk round in a circle;)
Jesus was born on Christmas day,
Christmas day, Christmas day,
Jesus was born on Christmas day,
Thank you, God, for Jesus.

This is the way we… buy the presents,
(mime the action)
…wrap the presents
…hide the presents
…give the presents
Thank you, God, for Jesus.

Carol
Blow the trumpet, bang the drum
CGC 40
Give out percussion instruments for the younger ones to play in the chorus of this song.

Story presentation
Copy suitable pictures on to OHP acetates – or large sheets of paper – and show them during the reading of 'Ellen's Surprise Present'. You could use articles, rather than pictures, for the presents or even live visual aids in the form of a mum and dad!

It was Ellen's birthday. She jumped out of bed and ran downstairs.

'Happy Birthday!' said her Mum, who was in the kitchen cooking eggs for breakfast.

'Happy birthday!' shouted her Dad, who was shaving in the bathroom.

Ellen was too excited to eat any breakfast. She watched at the window for the post to arrive, and when the postlady walked up the path, Ellen saw that she had lots of cards in her hand and a brown paper parcel.

She opened her cards and presents before she went to playgroup. Grandma had knitted her a lovely set of clothes for her special doll, Kim, and had made Ellen a matching sweater, too. The brown paper parcel was from her favourite uncle, who had sent her a beautiful story book with just the kind of pictures Ellen liked best. And Mum and Dad gave her a shiny, red bicycle with a basket on the front and a very loud bell. Ellen decided she would ride it to playgroup and ring her bell all the way.

Later that morning, on the way home, Mum asked, 'Did you say hello to Sugar and Spice this morning?' Sugar and Spice were Ellen's two gerbils, and she was very fond of them. They lived in a large fish tank in her bedroom. 'Oh dear,' said Ellen, 'I was so excited about my birthday, I forgot all about them. I didn't even give them any breakfast.'

'Don't worry,' said Mum, 'I fed them. But we'll go and see them when we get in: they have a surprise for you as well.'

When Ellen and her Mum got home they went upstairs to Ellen's bedroom. 'Be very quiet,' said Mum, mysteriously. Ellen crept over to the tank and looked in; there were Sugar and Spice and five tiny pink baby gerbils. 'Oh!' said Ellen, 'Sugar and Spice have given me a birthday present, too. I think it's the best one of all!'

Carol

The Virgin Mary had a baby boy MTB 39 or JP 251

Creative prayer-time

You will need a gummed coloured paper strip for each person in the congregation.

Ask everyone to think what they would like to give Jesus as a present on his birthday: the younger children will think very literally (eg a toy), so encourage them to give him something which is special to them. The older ones can be helped to think of more abstract things – helping someone, being kind, praying etc. Then ask them to write or draw their present on the gummed strip, and fasten it to their neighbour's, to make a paper chain. Sing together the verse from 'In the bleak mid-winter' beginning 'What shall I give him…' Ask three or four volunteers to bring the complete paper chain to the front of the church, and display it.

Say a prayer like, 'Lord, you gave us the best present of all when you sent Jesus to be born on the first Christmas day. Thank you that you love us so much. Please accept the gifts we bring to you.'

Carol

The rocking carol ('Little Jesus sweetly sleep' – in *The Oxford Book of Carols*) or 'Jesus, Baby Jesus' CS 18

Activity

Give everyone a piece of coloured card, roughly A5 size, folded in half. Working in groups of four or five, decorate the cards with crayons, felt tips, glitter, gold and silver stars etc.

The adults can help the children to write 'Happy Birthday Jesus' on the front, and 'with love from…' on the inside.

Ending

A blessing or dismissal of some kind should end the service. Keep it short, since it is important not to disrupt conversations arising out of the activity.

■ The Allabout sheet for this outline is on page 91.

■ PALM SUNDAY

This outline is the first of three, covering the events of Holy Week and Easter. It could be adapted to be used alone, but we suggest using it in conjunction with the Good Friday and Easter outlines, to complete the story. The visual display – a frieze – is planned to be built up over the three services.

■ **BIBLE LINK: Luke 19:28-40.**
■ **Focus for children:** Jesus was a king, but not the sort of king anyone expected.
■ **Focus for adults:** Jesus is a 'Saviour King' who can set us free from the oppression of sin, guilt and emotional pain. As King, he is worthy of our praise and honour.
■ **Theme:** following in the footsteps of Jesus the King.

In advance: prepare the frieze by copying the first part of the picture given with the outline for Easter. Judge how much room you have available for the whole frieze and draw your picture accordingly. (See page 17 for advice on enlarging pictures.) Colour-wash the sky in pale blue and the ground in yellow-brown. The city can be left white or coloured pale grey. You will also need to have ready sheets of coloured paper, scissors and sticky tape for other activities. (You will need plenty of green paper.)

■ OUTLINE
Song

We cry, 'Hosanna, Lord' CH 132 or Jesus said, 'Let's go into town!' LJI 84

Touch and talk

Have a display of pictures and items with a royal theme, eg pictures of kings and queens in stately robes, crowns, thrones, jewels – perhaps the Crown Jewels – and palaces. Can you find pictures of ancient kings and their palaces? Talk to the children about kings and queens. Where do they live? What do they do? Have the children ever been to a castle or a palace, or seen any member of the royal family?

Tell the children that gold is frequently used by kings and queens, and remind them that Jesus was given a gift of gold from one of the wise men who came to visit him as a baby. The gift of gold meant that Jesus, too, was a king. Today, they are going to learn some more about that.

Songs

Choose some lively songs that the children can do actions to, or accompany with percussion instruments.

*It's amazin' what praisin' can do IFW 38
* I will wave my hands IFW 43
Lord, you put some bounce in my feet IFW 59
* Jump! – in the *Jump!* songbook from TMC Records, 960 Gateway, Burlington, Ontario, Canada L7L 5K7.

Story presentation

• **Activity** – make some palm branches. Give each child a sheet of green A4 paper. Roll up the paper along the short side as tightly as possible and secure with sticky tape. Make cuts along the tube at one end, about 10cm long and close together to 'fray' it. Pull out the tube very gently from the middle so that the fronds separate slightly to look like branches of a tree.
When they have finished, ask them to keep their 'palms' safe for a little while, and go on to...
• **Tell the story**, using pictures on an OHP or flannel board, of Jesus asking his friends to bring him a donkey and then riding on it into Jerusalem. Explain how all the people shouted and cheered him, waving palm branches and spreading their cloaks on the ground for him.
• **Sing** 'He's off to Jerusalem' (LJI 82) and encourage the children to wave their palms during the chorus.
• **Act out the story** by gathering the children at the back and pretend to be the crowd who saw Jesus going into Jerusalem on a donkey. Say, 'Let's pretend we've seen someone coming. Who is it? It's Jesus…' and so on. As the children walk up to the front and wave their palm branches, encourage everyone to shout, 'Jesus is coming! Hooray for the king!' If you have the space, let the children form a procession. Give them shakers and

other instruments and encourage them to walk round while everyone sings...
• **Sing**: 'Praise God! Hallelujah!' LJI 83. Collect instruments and have the children sit down.
• **Explain** that Jesus wasn't the sort of king that the people were expecting. He wasn't going to build a palace and have lots of servants; he wasn't going to sit on a throne; he wasn't going to have a big army and fight battles. He wanted to be a king who helped people, who took care of them and who taught them to be kind and loving to one another.

Tell the children that some people were angry that Jesus wasn't going to be the sort of king they wanted, and in a few days' time they will hear what happened to Jesus next.

Song
We have a king who rides a donkey SSL 51

Creative prayer-time
• Give everyone two pieces of coloured paper, about A5 size. One should be green, to make a palm leaf; for the other, choose 'royal' colours, bright blue, red, emerald green, (Avoid purple and dark blue, because they will be needed for Good Friday, and gold and yellow, because they will be needed for Easter.)

Ask everyone to draw round their foot on the coloured piece of paper and cut it out, to make a footprint. Invite them to write a simple sentence on it – something like 'I will follow you' or 'Please, Jesus, walk with me.' (Younger children may just like to put their name on.)

Then ask them to draw a palm leaf shape on the green piece of paper and cut it out. They can 'frond' it as they did the trees earlier on. Invite them to write along the stem, 'Jesus is ....'s (name) King.'
• **Sing** again 'We have a king who rides a donkey' and ask everyone to stick their palm leaves and footprints on the frieze after the third verse. Sing the last verse more slowly and quietly as a prayer, in response to what has just been done.

Final songs
Choose songs of praise to close the worship, and encourage the children to wave their 'palm branches' or play instruments.

Oh, oh, oh, how good is the Lord JP 180
Praise him on the trumpet JP 200
Clap your hands all you people JP 26

Ending
A blessing or short dismissal should be used to end the time together.

Activity
This optional activity for the younger ones may be included after the prayer-time if time permits. Give each child a piece of thin card with a simple picture of Jesus riding on a donkey drawn on it. Have available glue, scraps of wool, fur fabric and material. Help the children to make a collage to take home.

■ The Allabout sheet for this outline is on page 91.

■ GOOD FRIDAY

It is not intended that this outline should stand alone but be used in conjuction with an Easter celebration, so that the children know the glorious end of the story. It is assumed that there may be older children present, too, so the age-range we have aimed at is about three to eight.

■ **BIBLE LINK: Mark 15.**
■ **Focus for children:** the story of Good Friday.
■ **Focus for adults:** Jesus' death was the reason for his life; by his death he opened the way for each of us to experience the forgiveness of God.
■ **Theme:** following in the footsteps of Jesus the Saviour.

In advance: on a large sheet of lining paper (or several sheets fastened together) draw the rest of the picture given with the outline on pages 68/69, keeping the colours as sombre as possible – black crosses, grey sky, dark shadows. (See page 17 for instructions on enlarging pictures.)

■ OUTLINE
Songs
Begin with two or three short, quiet songs, such as
Lord, we've come to worship you IFW 56
Jesus loves you and me (Jesus loves Kristi) FS 83
Jesus loves me, this I know JP 140

Touch and talk
Have ready a selection of seeds, bulbs, dead flowers, dead twigs – even a dead pot plant, to introduce the children to the idea of death and dying.

Encourage them to talk about plants and flowers dying. Cut flowers die quickly because they have been taken off the plant, other plants die at the end of the summer, plants will die through lack of water, leaves fall off trees in the autumn... etc. Invite some children to help make the plant material into a sad and lonely garden – using a tray of earth or sand. This garden should be kept: it will be transformed on Easter day!

Talk about how the plants leave

behind them the promise of new life to come in the form of seeds or bulbs.

Gently remind them that animals and people eventually die, too. Some of them may have experienced the deaths of their pets, or of members of their families. If they want to tell you, don't discourage them – small children need to talk about such things, and may well be discouraged from doing so at home.

Then explain that today is a very special, quiet day; it's called 'Good Friday' and it's the day when we remember about Jesus dying. Explain that although it was bad that Jesus had to die, we call it Good Friday because what happened afterwards was very good indeed, and that they will find out about that in a few days' time.

Song

Sing the first verse of 'I looked up and I saw my Lord a-coming' CH 36

Story presentation

The suggested story presentation is a mixture of listening, singing and activities, and it is important to use the material between this point and the responsive prayer as shown. **Tell the story** using OHP slides as visual aids.

In the week before Good Friday, Jesus had ridden into Jerusalem on a donkey and all the people had clapped and cheered him. They had spread their coats on the ground, waved palm leaves and shouted, 'Long live the King!' It had been very exciting!

But then, a few days' later, enemies of Jesus arranged for soldiers to arrest him and take him prisoner. They caught him one night when he was praying with his friends in a large garden.

His friends were very frightened. They didn't understand why Jesus had been taken away.

Then they heard that Jesus had been killed by being nailed to a cross. Jesus, their friend, was dead!

How sad they were! They thought they'd never see him again, but they were wrong. They would be seeing him very soon, but we must wait a couple of days for that exciting story!

Creative prayer-time

• Give everyone pieces of dark-coloured sugar paper – purple, black, grey, dark blue. Ask them to draw round their foot – adults or older children can help the little ones – and cut them out.

Explain that they are going to put their footprints on the frieze and ask them to choose where – on the paths between the city and the hill, or between the hill and the tomb. Invite all those who have chosen to put their prints between the city and the hill (children and adults) to stick them on the frieze. (Blu-tack is probably the easiest way of attaching them – they can be stuck on more firmly later if necessary.)

• Ask people to stay near the frieze after they have stuck on their footprints, and as a response **sing** together the second and third verses of 'I looked up...' (CH 36).

Continue with the story

(using OHP slides):

Jesus' friends were very, very sad. It seemed as if the whole world was sad, because the sun stopped shining and it went very dark.

When Jesus was dead, his friends took him down from the cross, wrapped his body in a long white cloth, and carried him to a nearby tomb – a small cave carved out of the rock.

They gently laid him in there and then rolled a large stone over the entrance. They said 'goodbye' to him and went away, sad and afraid, because their best friend, Jesus, was dead. He was no longer with them to help them.

Creative prayer-time

• Invite everyone who chose to stick their footprints on the path between the hill and the tomb to do so now. Ask them to stay near the frieze and together **sing** either two verses of 'Were you there when they crucified my Lord?' (JP 269) or 'Jesus is a friend of mine' including a verse 'Jesus died at Calvary' (JP 136).

• Ask everyone to return to their seats and conclude the prayer-time with this **responsive prayer**:

(*Leader*) Good Friday is a sad day:
(*All*) *Thank you for being with us when we are sad or afraid.*
(*Leader*) Your friends cried when you died:
(*All*) *Thank you for being with us when we are sad or afraid.*

(*Leader*) Your friends felt lonely when they said goodbye:
(*All*) *Thank you that you for being with us when we are sad or afraid.*
(*Leader*) Thank you that soon it will be Easter Day and the sadness will be over.

Activity

Give each child a clean half egg shell and some damp cotton wool. Help them to fill the shell with the cotton wool and then sprinkle on mustard seeds. Explain how to keep the cotton wool moist and to watch what happens to the seeds over the next few days. (On Easter day they can draw happy faces on the shell, and a few days later the 'hair' will grow.)

If you are planning to use the Easter outline on Easter Sunday, ask the children to bring their egg shells back with them when they come – without the faces.

Ending

Sing any suitable quiet song that the children know. End with a blessing or short dismisal.

■ The Allabout sheet for this outline is on page 92.

■ EASTER

■ **BIBLE LINK: John 20:1-18. Mary meets Jesus in the garden.**
■ **Focus for children:** Jesus is alive.
■ **Focus for adults:** the resurrection is the foundation of the Christian faith. By his resurrection, Jesus declares to us that we are loved and forgiven by God, and that we can know his love and power in our lives today.
■ **Theme:** following in the footsteps of the risen Jesus.

In advance: prepare the frieze made for Good Friday. Give a blue colour wash to the sky above the tomb; move the stone from in front of the tomb and add rays of light streaming from it.

■ OUTLINE
Songs
Begin the service with two or three short, lively songs of praise that the younger ones know well, then sing all of 'I looked up, and I saw my Lord a-coming' CH 36

Touch and talk
In advance, prepare a display of:
• sprouting pulses in various stages of development;
• budding twigs, showing green leaves, and twigs not yet beginning to grow – if you can find some!
• bulbs, some showing signs of growth – a sprouting onion bulb or a flower bulb beginning to shoot. (Amaryllis bulbs are very effective as the flower comes before the leaves.)

Let the children examine them, looking for roots, shoots etc, and comparing them with the dried pulses or seemingly dead twigs that you started with.

Talk about how the trees seemed dead until spring came and they began to shoot; how the dried beans and lentils were dead until they were given the right conditions to grow; how the bulb carries deep inside it the new flower for next season, and will start growing when it's buried in the ground.

Ask them if they can think of other examples of things in nature that seem dead but aren't, such as a seed, an egg, a chrysalis. What is alive inside each of them?

Explain to the children that today is a very special day because it is when we remember that Jesus, who died on Good Friday, came alive again on Easter Day!

Song
How do I know? LJI 88

Story
Explain to the children that eggs are special at Easter because they are the sign of new life. Read to the children how Haffertee found out all about chocolate Easter eggs in *The Easter Day Egg Hunt* from *Haffertee's First Easter* (Lion) pp 52–54, beginning from 'Why do we have chocolate eggs…'

Song
I'm alive! LJI 86

Story presentation
Use puppets to tell the story of Jesus' meeting with Mary in the garden after the resurrection. You will need only two puppets and the 'garden'.

Mary: I'm so sad… On Friday the best friend I ever had in the world died and we put him here in a tomb in this garden… That was awful, the worst day of my life.
But when I came to see him this morning he wasn't here! Somebody must have taken his body away and put it somewhere else, but I don't know where… Ohhh, I feel so unhappy.
(*Looks up and sees Jesus*)
Jesus: What's the matter?
Mary: Oh! Are you the gardener? Please, Sir, if you have taken my friend away, please tell me where you've put him…
Jesus: Mary, don't you recognise me?
Mary: Jesus…? Jesus! Is it really you? You're not dead after all! This is *wonderful*!
Jesus: Yes, I'm alive. Go and tell all my friends that I have come back to life, just as I said I would. Tell them I'll see them soon.
Mary: Yes, Jesus, yes I will. I can't wait to see their faces! This is the best day of my life!!

Song
My God is so BIG! CSM 30

Creative prayer-time
Give everyone a piece of brightly coloured sugar paper and ask them to cut round their feet (as in the outline for Good Friday). If they want to write their names on the footprints, they can do so.

Let everyone stick their footprints on to the path between the tomb and the city. (These represent joyful footsteps now that the tomb is empty and Jesus is alive.)

Give each child several circles of tissue paper in different colours, and help them scrunch them up together to make flowers, which they can stick along the path and near the tomb.

Let everyone stay where they are and say together:

(*Leader*) Your friends saw you were dead,
(*All*) *And they were sad.*
(*Leader*) But now you are alive,
(*All*) *And we are glad!*
(*Leader*) You are with us every day In our work and in our play,
(*All*) *Lord Jesus, you're the best friend we can have.*

(Alternatively, you could sing this prayer to the tune 'If you're happy and you know it, clap your hands'.)

Activities
• **Decorate an Easter garden**. Use the sad and lonely garden made on Good Friday. Have ready a variety of small plants and flowers, small twigs from shrubs etc. Let the younger children help to turn the sad and lonely garden into a happy, colourful one by decorating it with the flowers and twigs.
• **Make some happy faces**. The mustard seeds the children sowed in egg shells on Good Friday will be starting to sprout, and if they have remembered to bring them, now is the time to decorate them with felt tips. Let the children draw the happiest faces they can on the egg shells – in another few days the 'heads' will grow green 'hair'! On the back of the egg shells, help them to write 'Jesus is alive!' (Have lots of spare egg shells, damp cotton wool and seeds for those who have forgotten or were not at the Good Friday service.)

Ending

Conclude by singing 'We have a king who rides a donkey' SSL 51, or any other suitable Easter hymn, and an Easter blesssing or short dismissal.

■ The Allabout sheet for this outline is on page 92.

▪ PENTECOST

▪ **BIBLE LINK:** Acts 2:1-13 – the coming of the Holy Spirit.

▪ **Focus for children:** although we can't see God, he is always with us.

▪ **Focus for adults:** Jesus sent the Holy Spirit to take his place in the world. The Holy Spirit comes to us as our Helper, Comforter and Guide, and he makes us aware of the presence and power of Jesus in our lives. It is through the Holy Spirit that we come to faith.

In advance:

• Make a banner from a piece of material about 1m x 50cm. Turn under a hem along the longest edges and insert pieces of dowelling. Attach string so that it can be hung up. Cut out letters in felt or other non-fray material and stick on the words, 'The Holy Spirit helps us.'

• Cut out doves from white card with a slit in which to insert wings and have strips of tissue paper for the wings.

▪ OUTLINE
Songs

Begin with two or three short songs of praise, emphasising God's love, such as God's our Father LJI 8
* Jesus' love is very wonderful JP 139
This is the day JP 255
God is good JP 55

Touch and talk

This section is to help the children understand that some things are very real even though they cannot be seen, and to compare that with the fact that God can't be seen.

• **Air**: Ask the children to hold their hands up a little way from their faces, and then blow gently. What can they feel? Can they see anything coming out of their mouths?

• **Wind**: Ask the children to tell you about a windy day. What can they see on a windy day? Can they see the wind? No, only its effects.

• **Blowing bubbles**: Bring a 'Bubble Tub' to the service and blow some bubbles. What happens to the bubbles when they burst? If the children hold their hands near a bubble when it bursts, can they feel tiny drops of wetness on their skin? That's the liquid that the bubble was made from.

Explain that although we can't *see* God, we know he is there because of everything he does, just as we know that the air, the wind and the liquid that makes bubbles are still there.

Rhyme
Five little leaves so bright and gay TLP 89

Story presentation
Explain to the children that people who are special to us sometimes have to go away; perhaps they move to another house and it's not easy to see them anymore; perhaps they have to go away for a while because of their job. We know that they still care for us because they send us letters and cards, or phone us up, or perhaps even send us presents.

Jesus had to go away and leave his friends. But before he went away he promised them that he would send a very special present – the Holy Spirit – so that they would know he always loved them and would always be their friend.

Tell the story in Acts 2 (using OHP slides)

Jesus' friends were very sad and afraid. Jesus had gone away for good. He'd said goodbye to them and now they were all on their own. He'd promised to send them some help, but they didn't know what it would be or when it would come.

Now all the friends of Jesus were together in a big upstairs room. They had been talking about him and remembering all the things he had done. They wondered if they'd be taken prisoners by soldiers, too – just like Jesus a few weeks ago. (*Ask the children to tell you when this was.*) They were talking about the promise of special help Jesus had made to them and wondering what it meant.

Suddenly they heard a loud noise – just like a strong gust of wind. Somewhere downstairs a door slammed. The gust of wind swept through the house, up the stairs and blew open the door of the room where they were sitting.

The wind became stronger and stronger and as it did so, Jesus' friends began to feel warm and strong inside and could feel themselves getting

braver and braver. Little lights appeared above their heads, like tiny flames. They smiled and hugged each other. Everything was going to be all right! Jesus was still with them, even though they couldn't see him. He was still their special friend! They wanted to shout and dance. They were laughing and clapping and dancing for joy and shouting praises to God.

A huge crowd had gathered outside the house, wondering what was going on. Peter looked out of the window and saw everyone. 'I'm going to tell them about Jesus,' he said. So he stood up in front of the huge crowd and told them how much Jesus loved them – and that they could be his special friends, too.

Peter and his friends told everyone about Jesus. They weren't scared or worried any more. Something wonderful had happened to them, making them brave and very, very happy.

Songs
Choose from one or two praise songs such as:
Lord, you put a tongue
  in my mouth IFW 58
God is good JP 55
When the Spirit of the Lord
  is within my heart SHF 604

Creative prayer-time
Begin the prayer time by singing 'Remember Me' LJI 91
Then say this action prayer together.

Jesus friends were lonely and afraid.
  (*Curl up*)
Jesus friends were waiting for his help.
  (*Look around*)
Jesus sent his friends the Holy Spirit,
  (*Begin to stand up*)
To make them strong and brave and
  happy in his love. (*Stretch arms up high*)

Sometimes I am lonely and afraid,
  (*Repeat actions*)
Sometimes I am waiting for your help.
Thank you that you sent the Holy Spirit,
To make me strong and brave and
  happy in your love.

Banner
Give everyone either pieces of blue and white net to cut into cloud shapes, or red and yellow felt to cut into flames.

Let the children stick the pieces of

net on to the banner, overlapping them to give depth, and then stick the flames on top.

The leader can then hang the banner up in church and say a one-sentence prayer like: 'Thank you, Jesus, that you sent the Holy Spirit to help us.'

Song
Who can see the great wind blow?
  SSL 52

Activity
Explain that the dove is sometimes used to remind us of the Holy Spirit and give all the younger children a cut-out dove (minus wings), a piece of tissue paper and a length of shirring elastic. Help them to fold the tissue concertina-fashion along its length and slot it through the slit in the dove's body. Fan out the wings on each side and attach a piece of shirring elastic so that the dove will bounce up and down.

Ending
Finish the service by giving everyone a balloon and a piece of string. Let them use the air in their lungs to blow up the balloons, and then tie on the string. Holding the balloons, everyone sings 'Who can see the great wind blow?' again. Conclude with a bessing or dismissal.

■ The Allabout sheet for this outline is on page 93.

ALL ABOUT SHEETS

GOD MADE ME
EARS

Talkabout

• **Your child's ears,** and how amazing they are – they not only hear sounds but also locate them. They can hear someone talking to them even in a noisy place because they can shut off what they don't want to hear. People with normal hearing take these things for granted, but hearing loss often begins with the loss of these abilities.

• **Point out that because we can hear we can talk;** babies learn to talk by listening and copying, so deaf babies can't talk – they can only make noises. Tell your child about the hearing tests he/she had done as a baby. Deaf people also find it difficult to sing, either because they can't hear the notes of the music or because it all sounds the same.

• **Deaf and hearing-impaired people.** Ask someone you know to show you a hearing aid; explain that it works a bit like the volume control on the television, making sounds louder. (Unfortunately it makes all sounds louder, so doesn't always help in noisy places.)

• **Animals' ears and the ways in which they are adapted for the animal's life;** animals can usually move their ears much more than we can, and may have much more acute hearing. If you have a dog, notice that the dog hears things before you do. (Some deaf people living alone have dogs to tell them when the doorbell rings.)

• **Sign language** – an alternative to speech for deaf people. Point out that we all use some signs, eg waving, beckoning, a finger on the lips, nodding and shaking the head, pointing a finger…but that there is a whole language made up of signs.

Readabout

• *Little Beaver and the Echo* by Amy MacDonald (Walker Books, ISBN 0 7445 0443 0).

• **Find a book in the library about a deaf child** and read it together, eg *I Have a Sister; My Sister is Deaf* by Jeanne Whitehouse Peterson (Harper and Row, ISBN 0 06 024701 0).

Walkabout

• As you go about this week, **look for the Sympathetic Hearing Scheme logo** – a burgundy square with a stylised ear in white superimposed on a white diagonal. It's most often displayed in shops and banks to indicate that staff are prepared to help people who are hearing impaired. You may also see them at stations, in some restaurants and on phone kiosks.

• **Look to see how many different kinds of animal ears** you can spot this week.

• **Experiment with echoes** if there is somewhere suitable!

Howabout

• **Watching part of a signed TV programme for the deaf,** eg 'See Hear'. Notice how rapidly the signers can sign, and point out that though we can't understand it, many deaf people can.

• **Playing the listening game** – pause for a few seconds each day and see how many things you can hear. Your child may well hear more than you as children usually have very acute hearing.

• If your TV has Teletext, **bringing up the subtitles on a children's programme,** explaining that they are for deaf people.

Prayabout

• **Thank God together for the gift of hearing** each time you do something that depends on listening, eg enjoying a bed-time story, singing a favourite song, listening to a tape or a TV programme.

GOD MADE ME
MOUTH & TONGUE

Talkabout

Different shaped mouths. Talk about happy, sad, cross mouths (ie how feelings are shown). Play a game of *Guess Who?* (M&B games).

Readabout

• **Your sense of taste** in *Taste* by Wayne Jackman (Wayland, ISBN 1 85210 733 2).

• **Making sounds** in *Talkabout Sound* by Angela Webb (Franklin Watts, ISBN 0 86313 564 1).

Walkabout

Count happy faces. When you next go shopping, look out for the people who smile at you.

Howabout

• **Trying to eat a meal without talking;** use as many other different ways of communicating that you can!

• **Finding out about tongues.** Feel how rough a cat's tongue is. Why? What does a dog's tongue feel like? How many different kinds of tongues are there? What does a butterfly's tongue look like?

• **Playing a sound game with your child.** Take it in turns to make everyday sounds and try to guess what they are.

• **Doing an experiment.** Find out which parts of your mouth taste sweetness, sourness, bitterness and saltiness. Find a close-up picture of a tongue. Point out the taste-buds.

Prayabout

Say a grace before a meal. Make up your own, or say this one. You could think up some actions, too:

> *God, who feeds the robin,*
> *High up in the tree,*
> *Thank you for providing*
> *Lovely food for me!*

More graces can be found in *Everyday Graces* (Lion, ISBN 0 85648 030 4).

GOD MADE ME
NOSES

Talkabout
• **How animals use their sense of smell.** Observe animals you see. Watch a dog sniffing outside, or, if you have a dog of your own, observe how it sniffs you to get information about where you have been.
• Next time your child is helping you unpack the shopping, **encourage him/her to smell the items.** How many can he identify with his eyes shut?

Readabout
• **The first time Esau lost something to Jacob** because of a mouth-watering smell (Genesis 25:27-34).
• **How Pinocchio's nose grew longer** when he began to tell lies. (Your local library will probably have a suitable version of this story.)
• *Fox and Hen* by Helen Piers (Methuen) is the story of a fox who is distracted from lying in wait for a plump hen by the smell of newly-baked cakes.

Walkabout
Look for different noses on advertisements and posters. Count all the noses you can see in one morning or afternoon.

Howabout
• **Seeing how many different ways there are of sneezing!** Can your child recognise the people in your house by their sneezes?
• **Doing an experiment together.** Ask your child to shut her eyes. Hold a piece of pear under her nose, while she eats a piece of apple. Can she identify what she is eating? Talk about the connection between smell and taste.

Prayabout
Noses and our sense of smell. Let your child suggest the smells she wants to thank God for. Here is the sort of prayer you might pray:

Thank you, God,
for wonderful things to smell:
Thank you for cakes cooking,
and bacon frying;
For the fresh smell of the garden
after rain:
For the scent of flowers
and newly cut grass:
For the safe smell of my bed
and the people I love.
Thank you for noses
to smell with.

Prayabout
Each day this week stick onto a chart a small piece of something your child can feel – a piece of furry fabric, sandpaper, a piece of kitchen sponge, tissue paper, tinfoil, wood or pencil shavings, cotton wool or knitting wool, sheep's wool or feathers. **As you feel the things together, say thank you to God** for being able to touch and feel things, and for that amazing stuff called skin.

GOD MADE ME
FINGERS & SKIN

Talkabout
• **Skin:** perhaps at bath-time point out that it covers us all over and grows as we grow.
• **Has your child noticed any differences between** say their own skin and an old person's?
• **Is skin the same colour all over?**
• **Skin's special 'properties':** if we get hot we sweat; skin has tiny holes in it. If we get cold we get 'goose-pimples'. Through our skins we feel not only textures, but heat, cold and pain – a warning that something is wrong.
• **What happens to our skin if we stay in water for a long time?**
• **Words for different ways of feeling and touching** – tickle, stroke, rub, smooth and so on.

Howabout
• **Enjoying some finger-rhymes together.**
• **Doing some finger painting.**
• **Keeping a record for a week** of the different things we do with our fingers.
• **Simple sewing.** Ask for binca at the haberdashery counter if you want material with easy-to-see holes; use thick thread or wool and a large round-ended needle. Be prepared to re-thread the needle endlessly!
• **Touching and talking** about the texture of lots of everyday things.
• Going to the library and **finding out about skins of other creatures,** eg snakes and fishes.

HANDS & ARMS, LEGS & FEET

Talkabout

Take opportunities this week to **talk to your child about the amazing range of movements we can make with arms and legs.**

• What difference would it make if we didn't have knees and elbows?

• In how many directions can we move our hands, feet, arms and legs?

• Does your child know names like elbow, ankle, knuckle, palm, wrist, fist, heel?

• Look carefully together at your hands. Notice the nails and the knuckles; what are they for? What happens if we keep our fingers straight? What can't we do if we don't use our knuckles to bend our fingers?

• Talk about thumbs and how they increase the range of movements we can make.

• Consider the differences in size of hands in your family.

• What other groups of animals have 'arms' (monkeys and apes) and 'hands' (some rodents – squirrels, hamsters, gerbils)?

• Point out that other animals have four legs, not two arms and two legs, while birds have two legs and two wings.

• Talk simply about the way in which different animals' legs are adapted for the life they lead. Look at some picture books which show animals like kangaroos or rabbits.

• Talk about animals' feet – what different names do they have? Do they all have the same number of toes?

Walkabout

Play simple observation games as you are out this week.

• How many people can you count/see wearing shoes of a particular colour, or shoes with buckles?

• In winter, how many people are wearing gloves?

• How many different things are people doing with their hands and feet/arms and legs – eg driving a car, kicking a ball, cleaning windows, weighing out potatoes, typing, pushing a pram… If possible, watch someone repairing shoes – teach the words 'sole' and 'heel'.

• In winter, or in wet and muddy places, can you identify bird and animal footprints?

Howabout

• **Making a hand and foot chart** for all the family, and comparing the sizes. Whose are biggest? Whose are smallest?

• **Making an arm- and leg-length chart,** using pieces of string instead of centimetre measurements. Is it true that the person with the biggest feet has the longest legs?

• **Making puppets from gloves or paper bags** and putting on a puppet show from behind an armchair or sofa.

Prayabout

Make a list, perhaps with pictures, of all your child can do with their hands and feet and **use the list to say 'thank you' to God.**

EYES

Talkabout

• **Find a simple library book about the eye** and show your child the various parts of the eye, especially the pupil, which automatically changes size according to the amount of light available.

• **Tears,** about how the surface of the eye is continuously washed and kept clean and free from infection.

• **Why do we have eyelids and eyelashes?** What can you discover together about birds' eyelids? Why do camels have long eyelashes?

• **Find a picture-book of nocturnal creatures,** eg owls and lemurs; how are their eyes adapted for seeing at night?

• **If you have pets look at their eyes too;** what colour are they?

Readabout

• *Peepo* by Janet and Alan Ahlberg (Puffin ISBN 014 050384 6),

• *Ben's Brand New Glasses* by Carolyn Dinan (Faber & Faber ISBN 0 5711 4567 1),

• *Topsy and Tim have their eyes tested* by Jean and Gareth Anderson (Blackie).

Walkabout

• When you next go out, **notice how many people are wearing glasses.** Look in the window of an optician's shop and talk about what you can see.

• **Look out for blind people** with white sticks or guide-dogs.

• **If you are out in the car at night, point out the 'cat's eyes'.** This could lead on to a discussion of reflectors in general.

Howabout

• **Making a chart together** showing family eye colour. If possible include grandparents, cousins and aunts and uncles.

• **Collecting silver paper** for the Guide Dogs for the Blind Association.

• **Playing I-Spy,** using colours instead of initial letters.

• **Seeing how many words you know about eyes** and looking, eg wink, blink, look, see, watch, stare, spy….

Prayabout

There are some things we can only know by seeing, eg the idea of colour is almost impossible to explain to someone without sight. **Focus on colour at home this week;** perhaps you could make a small display of a particular colour, maybe your child's favourite, and say thank you to God for the most colourful thing you've enjoyed together each day. A rainbow has seven stripes; could you make a rainbow poster and each day for a week write in or draw something you've seen for which you can thank God?

Howabout

- **Making an animal poster or frieze** with pictures cut from magazines and cards.
- **Planning a day out at a zoo or safari park.** Choose a fairly small one, as under-fives have only limited powers of concentration and stamina.
- **Watching a wildlife documentary** with your child. They may not want to watch all of it, but most children are fascinated by good wildlife films.
- **Making a hedgehog cake,** using chocolate buttons or sticks for its prickles.
- **Making a hedgehog** with used matchsticks stuck into an oval potato.

Prayabout

Sing with your child any songs you know about animals, and thank God for them – perhaps a different one each day.

CREATION
WILD ANIMALS

Talkabout

- If your child seems interested, **talk about lions and tigers** belonging to the same family as domestic cats. Can you see a family likeness?
- **Talk about animals' coats** – hair, fur, scales, and their different ways of moving.

Readabout

- Most small children are fascinated by wild animals, and you may have both picture and story books about them. If not, help your child to choose some at the library, and look at them together; be guided in your conversation by the child's questions and comments. A story under-fives will enjoy is *Victoria and the Crowded Pocket* by Carolyn Sloan (ISBN 0 5821 6043 X) about a terribly untidy mother kangaroo who crams so many things into her pouch that her daughter leaves in disgust!
- Can your child give names to any pictures of native wild animals?

Walkabout

- As you go about this week, **see if you can spot squirrels in the trees in your park,** or see other wild animals.
- **Can you see any other pictures of wild animals?** Often animals are used in advertising, and it would be fun for children to try to spot them.

CREATION
BIRDS & THINGS THAT FLY

Talkabout

- **Feathers, birds' nests, birds hatching from eggs, dust baths.**
- Different birds have different sorts of **beaks** according to what they eat: get a simple illustrated book from the library to show your child these differences.
- **Tell your child about birdwatching.**
- **Other flying creatures** – bats and bees for instance. Does your child know that bees make honey?

Readabout

Read some of the following stories together: 'The ugly duckling' in a simple retelling, eg the Ladybird edition; 'The goose that laid the golden egg' – also in Ladybird; 'Elijah and the ravens' (from a child's Bible story book), and for four and five year old 'experienced listeners', perhaps *The Owl who was Afraid of the Dark*, by Jill Tomlinson (Young Puffin ISBN 0 14 030634 X) and *Jemima Puddleduck* by Beatrix Potter. The Ant and Bee books are always popular with small children and over fours would like a simple version of the fable 'The grasshopper and the ant'. Try *Spotter Puff* by Patricia Drew (Chatto and Windus, ISBN 0 7011 5053 X) or *The Very Hungry Caterpillar* and *The Bad Tempered Ladybird* by Eric Carle (Picture Puffins).

Walkabout

- **How many different birds can you spot this week?** Small children can't be still or quiet for long so watching from a window or visiting the nearest duck pond might be possible solutions. Ask a few questions to encourage close observation: How do birds walk? Can you walk like that? How do birds hold on to branches?
- **In autumn and winter look for old nests in the garden or in hedgerows,** but don't disturb in the spring and remember that it's illegal to remove birds' eggs. Can you find any birds' feathers? Can you recognise any bird calls?
- **In a park or garden can you find any flying things,** like ladybirds, or see any butterflies or bees?
- **Has your child ever seen a beehive?** Look out for them, eg on honey jar labels even if you can't spot real ones.
- **Encourage children to look for pictures/symbols of flying things,** eg the ladybird on Ladybird books and clothes, the puffin and penguin on other books.

Howabout

- **Visiting a bird park** – the smaller the better, as young children can't take in too much all at once. If you can't manage this, a small child gets enormous pleasure from a visit to a pet shop where there are birds in cages.
- **Making a bird table or bird feeder** from kitchen scraps and unsalted peanuts, mixed with melted lard and left to set in a cup or basin before being unmoulded and hung up for the birds. (Only feed birds in late autumn and winter.)

Prayabout

- **Make a chart** divided into seven sections labelled with the days of the week. Each day draw, paint or stick on something 'birdie' – a nest, with stuck on twigs, grass and moss, feathers, birds' eggs, a bird table, a fluffy chick, a bird cage and a wild bird.
- **Thank God for birds each day.** Draw a simple beehive shape divided into seven, and record each day what flying things (birds or otherwise) you have seen.

TREES & WOOD

Talkabout
- **Trees that lose their leaves in autumn and those that stay green all year round.**
- **Fruit trees.**
- **Trees as homes for birds and animals like squirrels**
- **Carpenters, joiners and the tools they use.** Jesus was a carpenter, so he would have known about making furniture.
- **Uses for wood:** furniture and toys, doors and window frames, boats.

Walkabout
- **As you go out this week, make a point of looking for and at trees;** if you live in a town, go to the park.
- **How many trees can you name?**
- **Look at the shape and colour of each tree;** notice the leaves and the bark, and things like cones, ash and sycamore keys, acorns, conkers etc.

Howabout
- Finding all the things made of wood in your house.
- Finding a tree that's safe to climb or a fallen tree trunk to balance on.
- Counting the rings on a sawn-off trunk to find the age of the tree.
- Lifting a piece of bark at the base of a tree and seeing the creatures beneath it.
- Shuffling through fallen leaves in autumn. (Talk about the sort of noise this makes.)
- Planting an acorn or conker in a jam-jar or plant pot and watching it grow.
- Making a collection of pine-cones and displaying them at home; you could paint some or make a pine-cone family. Closed up cones can be made to open by putting them in a very slow oven, on a baking sheet, for an hour or so; the aroma is lovely, and when you next pick them up, there will be a shower of tiny light seeds – also fascinating to a small child.

Prayabout
Make a small collection of 'tree' things this week. Display it as attractively as possible – perhaps on a brightly coloured cloth or crepe paper – so that your child feels it's important, and thank God every day for trees and all the things we are able to make from wood.

FLOWERS & PLANTS

Talkabout
- Be guided, as always, by your child's level of interest and understanding, but show her the **different parts of a flower – petals, leaves and stem.** Show her something like a foxglove which has lines to guide the bees in to collect nectar to make honey.
- **Plant roots,** if possible showing some, and explaining that the roots take in water from the earth and send it to the other parts of the plant.
- **All the different shapes of leaves, and their textures** – some are glossy, some rough, some hairy, but nearly all are green.
- **The different colours of flowers and plants** – spring flowers are predominantly yellow, while blossom is usually pink or white. Which colour flower is your child's favourite?

Walkabout
- **As you go out this week, look at gardens** – big ones, small ones, even ones in window boxes. If you live in an area where gardens are impossible, could you manage an outing to a local park?
- **How many different kinds of flowers and plants can you spot** in one particular area? How many people have flowers or plants in their windows? (Small children love this kind of spotting game.)

Howabout
- **Doing some simple flower/leaf/ornamental grass pressing?** Choose well-formed, dry flowers and place them between absorbent paper, under a heavy weight, for a couple of weeks. Put them out of your child's way or they will be constantly tempted to peep. Use the pressed flowers to make a special card, perhaps for a grandparent.
- **A small experiment:** put some pale single-colour flowers in a jar of water to which you have added food colouring (of a different colour to the flowers). After a day or two talk to your child about what has happened to the flowers.
- **Making a garden with your child:** even if you haven't a proper garden, you can grow plants indoors, or on a window-sill, and children get enormous pleasure from watching things they have planted begin to grow. If you plant seeds, read the back of the packet and find ones that will germinate fairly quickly.

Prayabout
Use this prayer with your child this week:

'Dear God, thank you for making so many beautiful flowers and plants. Amen.'

GOD GIVES US
BREAD

Talkabout

• **Talk to your child about where bread comes from.** If you live in the country go and look at a field of wheat, or even an old windmill if there is one near you. If you live in a more urban setting, find a book about bread in the children's section of the library and talk about it together.

• **How many kinds of bread** does your child know?

• **What happens to the texture of bread when you make toast?**

Walkabout

• **Look in the windows of a baker's shop,** or at the bakery section of a large supermarket. Talk about the different kinds of bread you can see; could you buy a different kind of loaf for a change? For example you could buy a loaf with grains in it and talk about their appearance and texture.

• Ducks like bread too! **Have an outing to feed the ducks.**

Howabout

• **Making bread at home!** It's really very easy – especially if you use 'easy-blend yeast' which is added to the dry ingredients, and 'strong' flour, sold in most supermarkets as bread flour, which is always plain. Wholewheat by itself can be a little 'heavy' for a child so a mixture of half brown and half white is usually best.

• **Obtaining some grains of wheat or barley,** eg from a pet shop or a health food shop, and looking at them carefully. Can you find a way to grind them up? (Let your child make suggestions.) What do you get?

• **Making a pattern or picture** by gluing grains to a piece of strong paper.

• **Sowing some grain in a shallow box or tray** and watching it grow.

Prayabout

Make **a pictorial chart showing how much bread your child eats each day** – or at what meals. Sing

Thank you for the food we eat,
Bread and butter, milk and meat.
Fruit and fish the boats bring in,
Thank you, God, for everything.

each time you have bread this week.

GOD GIVES US
WATER

Talkabout

• **Where does your water at home come from?** How many taps have you got? How many hot and how many cold? Where does the water go when we've finished with it? How does it get into the taps?

• Many people in the world don't have water in taps – they have to fetch it from a tap in the street, or a well, or sometimes have to walk a long way to get it from a lake or river. You might **find some pictures of this** in library books.

• Our water is clean – we can drink it straight from the tap if we want to. Sometimes, especially in hot countries, water is dirty, or it looks clean but has lots of germs in it which make people very ill, especially small children.

• **Water sources:** rain, lakes and ponds, rivers and the sea. Explain the word 'reservoir'. Sea water is salty. Other water we call freshwater.

• **How many water words can you think of?** (Splash, shower, sprinkle, drench, sopping wet etc.)

Readabout

Books about water are plentiful, from books for very young children about bathtime to those for older pre-schoolers like *Tariq Learns to Swim* by Hassina Khan (Bodley Head, ISBN 0 370 30530 2), *Topsy and Tim's paddling pool* by Jean and Gareth Anderson (Blackie) or *Mrs Lather's Laundry* by Allan Ahlberg (Viking Kestrel, ISBN 0 670 80581 5).

Walkabout

• As you go out this week **look for ways of getting and storing water.** It's still possible to see old pumps in certain places; does your child know how to work one? Wells are less common, but if you do know of one, it would be worth a visit. What about water-butts in gardens, fountains, and drinking-troughs for horses, still seen in some cities?

• **Look out for people using water in their work:** window cleaners, firemen, the car-wash at the garage, and so on.

Howabout

Letting your child play with water more than usual – pouring and measuring, floating and sinking activities, all help him/her to understand the 'properties' of water. These can be done in the bath to cut down on mess. Allow experiments with food colouring, and let him/her paint.

Prayabout

Make a water mobile. At the top suspend a rain cloud, then underneath hang pictures of things which symbolise what you use water for – a tumbler shape, a shampoo bottle shape, a washing-machine shape etc. Thank God every day for his gift of clean water, and pray for people who don't have enough, or who have to walk miles to get it.

Thank you, God,
for giving us water to…
Please help people who don't
have enough. Amen.

GOD GIVES US
FRUIT & VEGETABLES

gardens, greengrocers' shops, supermarkets and markets. Encourage him to name as many as possible. Can you try a fruit you've never had before? Look at tins of fruit and vegetables as well as fresh ones.

Talkabout

- **All the different fruits and vegetables you use** and the different forms in which they come – fresh, frozen, canned, dried.
- **Which fruit and vegetables grow in this country** and which come from other countries and why.
- **How they grow** – in the ground, on bushes or trees, or on vines.
- **Find pictures of a 'hand' of bananas** (why is it called a hand?) or pineapples growing close to the ground.
- **Seeds and pips:** do all fruits have them? Can you grow some? (Pips are hard to germinate but children like to try. You are most likely to be successful if you plant a dry pip in damp potting compost, put a polythene bag secured with an elastic band over the pot, and leave it in the airing cupboard.)
- **Cooking fruit and vegetables.** Some we can eat raw; others have to be cooked. Some are sweet; others, like lemons, always sour.

Readabout

- *Apple Pigs* by Ruth Orbach (Fontana Picture Lions, ISBN 0 00 661403 5), is an amusing tale in verse about a neglected apple tree.
- 'The Garden Gang' (Ladybird) is a series of amusing books about fruits and vegetables.

Walkabout

Wherever you go this week encourage your child to **look for fruit and vegetables** –

Howabout

- **Making a salad** – fruit or vegetable or together.
- **Growing some carrot tops** on a saucer of water.
- **Planting a broad bean or runner bean in a jam jar and watching it grow.** (Put several layers of soggy kitchen paper round the sides of a jam jar. Put a bean between the side of the jar and the paper and keep it well watered.)
- **Planting some radishes.**
- **Making a picture** with lentils, split peas etc, glued onto a simple shape.

Prayabout

- **Make a collage** using pictures of fruits and vegetables cut from magazines. Write on it 'Thank you, God, for all these good things.'
- **Teach your child** 'All good gifts around us'

  All good gifts around us,
  Are sent from heaven above.
  Then thank the Lord,
  Oh thank the Lord,
  For all his love.

- **Use this grace** (to the tune 'Thank you for the world so sweet'):

  Thank you for the food we eat,
  Bread and butter, milk and meat,
  Fruit, and fish the boats bring in,
  Thank you, God, for everything.

GOD GIVES US
MILK & DAIRY PRODUCTS

Talkabout

- **Ways in which you use milk in your home.**
- **Milk as the staple food for young babies**, both human and those of other animals.
- **Cats like milk and cream – so do birds**, which is why sometimes the milk tops are pecked.
- **Why milk is good for us** – especially for children. It has calcium for strong teeth and bones, and protein for growth.
- **How milk gets to us from the farm** – from cow to tanker to industrial dairy to milkman/shop. You could probably find a suitable library book with pictures of the whole process.

Readabout

Older pre-schoolers would enjoy the poem 'The King's Breakfast', by A A Milne, found in numerous anthologies, and the Shirley Hughes story about a milkman, 'Mr McNally's Hat', in *The Big Alfie and Annie Rose Story Book* (ISBN 0 09 975030 9).

Walkabout

- When you go shopping look for the dairy **products in your shop or supermarket** – why are they in a chilled cabinet?
- **How many different kinds of cheeses** can you spot? How many have you tasted? Where do they all come from? All cheese is made with milk, but not necessarily cow's milk. Can you find a cheese made from goat's milk?

- **Is it possible to watch cows being milked somewhere?** If you can't do this immediately, bear it in mind for a day out, or on holiday, or watch for farm open days.

Howabout

- **Making some butter.** You need some fresh cream (or top of the milk – which takes longer), lots of patience, and a small screw-topped glass jar (sterilised). Put the cream in the jar; screw the lid on tightly and shake and shake and shake… Just when you think nothing is going to happen the cream turns into butter, with a watery liquid (buttermilk) left. Pour that off and use your butter – you may prefer it with a little salt.
- **Making yoghurt.** You need a pint of UHT (whole) milk, a teaspoon of live yoghurt (or a spoonful from the previous batch). Warm the milk until it is lukewarm (about 37°C) before whisking in the yoghurt. Put it into a clean bowl and leave covered for 24–36 hours; an airing cupboard is ideal. Keep it in the fridge and flavour as you wish.
- **Making a milk pudding** – bread and butter pudding, blancmange, rice pudding.

Prayabout

Draw a cow at the top of a large piece of paper, and write 'Thank you, God, for cows that give us milk'. Have a space for each day, and at bed-time think of all the things you've eaten or drunk that are made from milk. Fill in one each day, and say thank you to God for that.

GOD GIVES US
FAMILIES

Talkabout

Talk to your child about your own family.

• **Your parents.** Small children often realise the connection between parents and grandparents, but don't always realise that uncles and aunts are parents' brothers and sisters. Old photographs often help here.

• **Your own childhood experiences –** children love to hear about these, especially the naughty things you did! Talking in this way helps a child to understand something of the passage of time – a very difficult concept for under-fives – and also gives a sense of continuity, and of belonging, both of which are very important to a sense of security and general well-being.

• **Show your child any belongings –** perhaps books or toys – you still have from your childhood, or remind her that the farm she likes to play with at Grandad's used to be Daddy's when he was a little boy.

Readabout

• The 'Happy Families' series by Allan Ahlberg and Joe Wright (Puffin/Kestrel) are short and amusing stories about various non-stereotyped families: *Miss Jump the Jockey*, *Master Salt the Sailor's Son*, and *Mrs Plug the Plumber*, to name a few.

• *The Trouble with Jack* by Shirley Hughes (Bodley Head, ISBN 0 370 01514 2).

Walkabout

Look for other families as you go about this week. Look for families doing things together – perhaps doing the shopping, or taking a dog for a walk, or young families on the swings in the park, or out for a walk together on Sunday afternoon. Notice that some families may have grandparents with them.

Howabout

• **Helping your child make a 'My family' scrapbook.** Buy one or make one with strong paper folded or stitched, or use a cheap 'self-adhesive' photo album. Into this help your child put photos or his own pictures of members of your family, perhaps adding a brief description like, 'This is Aunty Sue – she has a ginger cat.'

• **Playing a family guessing game.** Take it in turns to give clues for the other person to guess which member of the family you're thinking about.

• **Making a family mobile.** Draw pictures or stick photos of family members on ovals of card, and suspend them from a coat-hanger.

Prayabout

Use the scrapbook (see above) or the family photo album, and **pray for different members of the family each day,** thanking God for them, and asking him to help them.

GOD GIVES US
MUSIC

Talkabout

The kind of music you and your children enjoy. Do you listen to your favourite music on TV, cassette tapes, the radio etc?

Readabout

Bertie and the Bear by P Allen.

Walkabout

Visit a shop that sells musical instruments. Identify the instruments with your child. If you are there when it's quiet, the staff will probably be very willing to talk to your child about the instruments on display.

Howabout

• **Making a glass harmonica.** Collect eight empty milk bottles and fill them with water to different levels. Each bottle will make a different note when tapped carefully with a wooden spoon handle. See if you can make a scale by varying the water level, then try out some simple tunes together.

• **Making a simple tambourine** out of a paper plate and some milk bottle tops. Let your child decorate a plain white paper plate with crayons or paints, then help him/her to staple milk bottle tops in pairs round the edge. The tops jingle when the 'tambourine' is shaken.

• **Finding out about the instruments of the orchestra** by listening to a record like Prokofiev's Peter and the Wolf suite. Young children enjoy the story, and soon learn to identify the different tunes used for each character.

• **Having a sing-song with your child.** It's great fun to sing action songs together or sing nursery rhymes and songs accompanied by clapping, home-made instruments etc. If you can play an instrument, such as piano or guitar, there are several books of songs available with simple accompaniments. A & C Black publish *Okki Tokki Unga* (a book of action songs), *Apusskidu* and *Ta-ra-ra-boom-de-ay* (both full of very singable songs).

Prayabout

Try using songs instead of prayers at your child's bed-time.

GOD GIVES US
HOMES

Talkabout

- **Your own home.** What is it built from? How is it heated? How long have you lived there?
- **Other houses your child is familiar with.** How is it different from your house? (You will probably be surprised at how much your child can tell you!) What is your address?
- **How are houses built?**
- **Can you visit a building site** – at a safe distance – or even look at a house where there is an extension being built? Does your child know words like 'foundations' and 'scaffolding'?

Howabout

- **Making houses from boxes and cartons** – perhaps painting them and adding roofs from folded rectangles of card.
- **Letting your child make a house for himself** from a large cardboard box, or the table covered with an old sheet. In good weather, a sheet over a climbing frame makes a good tent.

Prayabout

Each day, **thank God for your home** and for one particular room, eg the kitchen, where we can prepare food; the bathroom, where we can play with water and get clean; the bedroom, where we can sleep and rest… Ask God to bless your home and the homes of those you love, making them truly happy places.

Readabout

The Three Little Pigs (traditional), available in Ladybird, *The House that Jack Built* (traditional), a lovely version by Pam Adams is published by Child's Play, *Moving Molly* by Shirley Hughes (Collins, ISBN 0 00 661782 4) and *Sally's Secret* by Shirley Hughes (Picture Puffins).

Walkabout

- As you go out this week, **look again at all the houses** in your neighbourhood; point out the different colours of the bricks or stone and roof tiles, the different styles of chimney pots, and doors and windows. If there are old houses near you, look for things like boot scrapers at the front door, and places where the coal used to be tipped into the cellar.

GOD GIVES US
ANIMALS TO CARE FOR

Talkabout

How we get wool from sheep, and trace its journey through to your child's favourite jumper. Read *The Helen Piers Animal Story Book* (Methuen) with your child.

Walkabout

- **Visit local pet shops and animal shelters.** Most staff are very willing to talk about their animals if you catch them when they aren't busy.
- **Count the number of cats and dogs you see** on your way home. What colours are they? Can you name different breeds? (Warn young children about the dangers of approaching strange dogs.)
- **Look for spider's webs.** Look at the beautiful pattern of the webs, and try to find the spider. Has she caught any flies? She doesn't get stuck in her web because she only uses the 'spokes', and they aren't sticky.

Howabout

- **Making a bird table.** Put out food each winter day – scraps of fat, peanuts, raisins and crumbs of stale bread will attract a variety of garden birds. How many can you and your child identify?
- **Making a bird pudding.** Kitchen scraps set in melted fat in a small pudding basin or half a coconut shell make an excellent food source for birds in winter. Try hanging it up near a window, and watch the tits' acrobatics.
- **Finding out about caterpillars and butterflies.** Perhaps you can find a caterpillar on a cabbage leaf, and keep it until it emerges as a butterfly? Read *The Very Hungry Caterpillar* (Eric Carle, Picture Puffins) with your child.

GOD GIVES US
CLOTHES

Talkabout
- **Your child's clothes** as he/she gets dressed and undressed this week. What is each piece of clothing for? Where did you get it? What clothes are favourites and why? Why do clothes wear out? What do you do with things children outgrow?
- **Textures** – rough, smooth, shiny, warm or cold to the touch.
- **How many different ways of fastening a ciothe** can you discover?
- **What materials are used;** where do they come from; can you trace them back to God?

Readabout
Stories about clothes: *The Emperor's New Clothes* (traditional) *Alfie's Feet* by Shirley Hughes (Collins, ISBN 0 00 662161 9), *Postman Pat's Washing Day* by John Cunliffe (André Deutsch, ISBN 0 233 98297 3), *All In One Piece* by Jill Murphy (Walker Books, ISBN 0 7445 0749 9), *You'll Soon Grow into it, Titch* by Pat Hutchins (Bodley Head).

Walkabout
As you are out and about this week look for:
- **people in uniform** – supermarket staff, nurses, schoolchildren
- **people wearing special clothes for special jobs** – dustmen, dentists, telephone engineers.
- **clothes shops.**
- **footwear for different activities.**

Howabout
- **Letting your child do some washing:** use a mild handwashing detergent and give the child something fairly resilient but dirty so that he/she has the satisfaction of seeing the dirty water! Talk about rubbing and rinsing, and maybe find pictures of people washing clothes by the river in a hot country.
- **Starting a dressing-up box** if you haven't one already.
- **Looking at family photographs** to see what sort of clothes you wore as a child and to look at 'special occasions', like weddings, to see what people are wearing.

Prayabout
- **Thank God each day for some piece of clothing,** eg anoraks on a cold day, wellingtons on a wet day, or for the resources from which clothes are made.

GOD GIVES US
FISH

Talkabout
Ways of catching fish: rod and line, trawlers, small fishing boats. Ask at your local library for suitable books.

Readabout
- *Jeremy Fisher* by Beatrix Potter (Frederick Warne) tells how Jeremy nearly gets caught by a trout.
- *Topsy and Tim at the Seaside* by Jean and Gareth Anderson (Blackie).

Walkabout
- Next time you are in your local supermarket or fishmonger, **see how many different sorts of fish there are.** Large supermarkets have an enormous variety these days.
- **Visit a pet shop which specialises in tropical fish.** Marine tropical fish are especially beautiful.

Howabout
- **Buying a fishing net and taking your child to a local pond or stream to fish.** As long as they are closely supervised this is a lovely activity for a small child. It is an opportunity to learn about other small animals that live in or near water, too.
- **Buying a couple of goldfish.** They are very cheap to buy and small children enjoy watching them and helping to care for them.
- **Making a silver fish from milk bottle tops.** Cut out two large fish shapes from strong paper or card. Give your child some good quality glue and lots of clean, flattened milk bottle tops. Help him/her to stick them in an overlapping pattern on the fish, to look like scales. Make the eyes out of paper, or dried beans. Place the two shapes together and staple part of the way round, leaving an opening big enough to stuff with newspaper. Close the gap, attach a thread and hang up – perhaps in an old orange or lemon bag.

Prayabout
Next time you have fish and chips for tea, **sing this grace** (to the tune, 'Three blind mice'):

Fish and chips, fish and chips.
Vinegar and salt, vinegar and salt.
God gives us lovely things to eat,
Lots of lovely things to eat,
Hot and cold, salty and sweet,
Thank you, God.

FRIENDS

Talkabout

Other friends your child may have. Some children have imaginary friends; others have teddies which are very special friends; some children may see a family pet as a special friend; many include adults among their friends. Depending on the age of your child, this may be an opportunity to warn him/her about the potential danger in assuming that all adults are friends.

We can say NO! by David Pithers and Sarah Greene (Beaver Books/NCH) is a book for parents to read to and discuss with 3s – 7s about keeping themselves safe from potentially dangerous adults.

Readabout

- **Haffertee**, the little soft toy hamster, who is Diamond Yo's special friend and who finds lots of friends of his own – including God. *Haffertee Hamster Diamond* by Janet and John Perkins (Lion).
- Other books about friends are *Little Beaver and the Echo* (Walker Books, ISBN 0 7445 0443 0) and *Best Friends for Frances* by Russell Hoban (Scholastic Publications, ISBN 0 590 70277 7).

Walkabout

On your way home, or the next time you are out, **count how many friends' houses you pass.** Wave to your friends if you see them.

Howabout

- **Inviting some friends to tea?** Perhaps your child can help with some of the preparation – making small cakes or laying the table.
- **Sending home-made cards** to let friends who live a long way away know you're thinking of them? The simplest cards can be made from old greetings cards cut out and mounted on plain coloured card.

Prayabout

At bed-time, help your child to pray for some of his/her friends by name. A very simple prayer would be:

Please, God, be with ...
tonight and keep them safe.

Howabout

Making a 'Special People' photograph gallery? Collect together snapshots of family, friends etc. It is possible to buy a large photo frame with spaces for up to a dozen photos, or else make a simple mount with your child's help.

Prayabout

Members of your family using a perspex photo cube. Roll the cube, as if it were a dice. Pray for the person whose photo is uppermost. Small children will enjoy this novel way of praying; a prayer as simple as, 'Please, Jesus, bless....' is enough.

PEOPLE WHO CARE FOR US

Talkabout

The people who are significant in your child's life – family, neighbours, family friends, nursery school teachers, health visitors etc. What about saying a prayer for them at bedtime?

Readabout

• *Alfie Gives a Hand* by Shirley Hughes (Bodley Head) tells how Alfie's apprehensions disappear when he takes care of someone else.

• *Topsy and Tim's Babysitter* by Jean and Gareth Adamson (Blackie) is a reassuring story about Mum and Dad going out.

• **Haffertee**, a soft toy hamster, who learns that God cares for him as well as the people he lives with. *Haffertee Hamster Diamond* by Janet and John Perkins is published by Lion.

Walkabout

Visit some adults who enjoy your children's company. It is very affirming to small children to be liked by adults outside the family – and very affirming to adults to be liked by small children! Perhaps they could take a small present?

PEOPLE WHO NEED OUR HELP

Talkabout

Life in poorer countries. What would you have for breakfast? Where would water come from? What sort of house would you live in? Perhaps a book from the library will help.

Readabout

How everyone helps when Mum's out in *Helpers* by Shirley Hughes (Picture Lions).

Walkabout

Your house and find things to take to a charity shop. You might buy something from the shop too.

Howabout

• **Having a different sort of meal** – Indian, African, Chinese. Are there special ways to eat this food?

• **Visiting someone who is lonely or needs some help?**

• **Finding out about sponsoring a needy child in another country.**

Prayabout

Give your child a piece of paper and encourage them to draw a picture of someone who they think needs help. When the picture is finished, ask Jesus to be with the person in the drawing and to help them.

Howabout

Doing a 'good turn' this week with your child. Perhaps he/she would like to colour a picture about it.

Prayabout

People who need Jesus' help. At bedtime, encourage yor child to name anyone they know who needs help and to say a simple prayer like: 'Please, Jesus, help…'.

PEOPLE

PEOPLE JESUS HELPED: 2

Talkabout

Different ways of helping. How do you help each other at home? Are there any friends or neighbours that you regularly help, or who help you? What is your child's experience of help and helping?

Readabout

• **More times when Jesus helped people.** Palm Tree books are enjoyable and inexpensive. Each book retells a story from the Bible in a straightforward way, with brightly coloured illustrations.

• *Helpers* or *Alfie Gives a Hand* (both by Shirley Hughes, published by Bodley Head).

Walkabout

Look out for people helping others, eg the school traffic wardens, fire engines and ambulances, staff who pack shopping in a supermarket, people helping in a market research survey, police, etc.

PEOPLE

PEOPLE JESUS HELPED: 1

Talkabout

Weddings, using words like husband and wife. Perhaps you have some photos of weddings you could show your child.

Readabout

• **What happens to Alfie** when he's invited to a party without Mum or Rosie, in *Alfie Gives a Hand* by Shirley Hughes (Bodley Head).

• 'Here Comes the Bridesmaid' in *Out and About* by Shirley Hughes.

• *When Willie Went to the Wedding* by Judith Kerr (Fontana Picture Lions, ISBN 0 00 661340 3).

Walkabout

Look out for weddings. You may see the bridal party standing outside a church having photographs taken. See if you can see confetti lying around church grounds after weddings. Photographers often have wedding photos in their windows. Dress shops may display a wedding dress.

Howabout

• **Finding out about wedding customs in different parts of the world.** Do you know any Jewish, Muslim or Hindu families? Ask them to tell your child about their weddings.

• **Making some gingerbread people.** Give your child some scraps of material and help him/her dress up a couple as a bride and groom. Enjoy the rest for your tea! Use your favourite recipe or the one below:

8oz (225g) plain flour
1.5 tsp (7.5ml) ground ginger
1.5 tsp (7.5ml) bicarbonate of soda
2 tblsp (30ml) golden syrup
2oz (50g) castor sugar
1.5oz (30g) margarine
1 egg, beaten
Currants for eyes, buttons

Sift the dry ingredients into a mixing bowl. Melt the syrup, sugar and margarine gently in a pan. Cool slightly, then stir into the flour, adding enough beaten egg to make a stiff dough. Roll out the dough until it is about a quarter of an inch thick, then cut out gingerbread people. Place on greased baking sheets, add currants for eyes and buttons. Bake at 350°F (Mark 4, 180°C) for about 15 minutes.

Prayabout

Draw a simple boy/girl shape on a piece of paper or thin card for your child. Let him/her colour it, then write, 'Jesus, you help me to …' Encourage your child to add something that Jesus helps him/her to do, each day for a week.

POSTMEN & POSTWOMEN

Talkabout

All the letters which come to your house in a week. See if you can count them all.

Readabout

• Postman Pat and his cat Jess. The stories from the television series are now in book form (André Deutsch).

• *Katie Morag Delivers the Mail* by Mairi Hedderwick (Picture Lions, ISBN 0 00 662432 4).

Walkabout

• On the way home, **count all the postboxes you can see.** Find out about posting times. Are there different kinds of postboxes?

• **Look at different letterboxes on houses.** (Some are high, some low, some are vertical, some horizontal, some are shiny....) How many different sorts can you spot?

Howabout

• **Starting a simple stamp collection.** Use an inexpensive stamp book or an exercise book. Even young children can have pleasure in collecting stamps off the letters which come to their house.

• **Finding out about the Post Office near your home.** What does it sell besides stamps? What is the name of your Postmaster/mistress? Find out how to post a parcel or a letter to another country.

Prayabout

All the people who work for the Post Office. Say a prayer at bedtime asking God to be with them, or use this prayer:

Thank you, God, for letters and cards,
And parcels that come on special days.
Thank you for the people who work,
Bringing our post in different ways.

Walkabout

When you are out, **listen for sirens and look out for ambulances.** Say a prayer together for the people in the ambulance. Look for disabled people in wheelchairs, with white sticks etc, and for people with limbs in plaster.

Howabout

• **Making a simple first aid kit together.** You will need plasters, bandages, gauze, antiseptic lotion/cream, sting cream, tweezers, scissors, cotton wool, surgical tape. Explain what each item is used for. Make sure it is kept well out of reach when it is finished.

• **Making a doll's hospital.**

Prayabout

At bedtime, **remember people who are sick.** Perhaps you would like to pray one of these prayers with your child:

Lord Jesus, sometimes I'm not well.
Thank you for all the people who care
   for me and help me to get better.
Please look after all the sick people
in hospitals, and help the people who
   care for them.

Lord, when I hear an ambulance siren
it means that someone is very sick.
   Please look after them.

DOCTORS, NURSES & HEALTH VISITORS

Talkabout

• **The care people need when they are not well:** special food, medicines, etc. Sometimes people need to go to hospital for extra special care.

• **Hospital; especially if your child was born in one.** Talk about different kinds of nurses: health visitors, midwives, dental nurses, school nurses.

• **Doctors and hospitals.** *Going into Hospital* by Althea is very reassuring; so is *Topsy and Tim go to the Doctor's* by Jean and Gareth Anderson (Blackie).

Readabout

• *Rachel* by Elizabeth Fanshawe (Bodley Head, ISBN 0 370 10738 7) is about a child in a wheelchair and is good for helping children form positive attitudes towards disabled people.

• *The Check-up* by Helen Oxenbury (Walker Books, ISBN 0 7445 0038 9) has an amusing twist to it!

SUN

Talkabout

• **The sun** – giving us light and heat and helping plants of all kinds to grow, and ripening fruit.

• **Summer and winter** – the differences, and about hot countries and cold countries.

• Have you had **a summer holiday** away from home? What did you do? How much can your child remember?

• **Effects of too much sun** – on people (sunburn and sunstroke) and on growing things (crop failure).

• Would your child be interested in **a thermometer?** Talk about sundials and the idea of people telling the time by the sun, which actually small children still do without realising it – 'It's not dark so it's not bedtime!'

Howabout

• **Going to a pick-your-own fruit farm.** Point out the differences between ripe and unripe fruit – in colour, texture and taste. Unripe raspberries for example are green, hard and sour; ripe ones are pink, soft and sweet.

• **Experimenting with ripening green fruit indoors,** eg tomatoes or bananas, pointing out that it's the warmth of the sun which ripens fruit naturally.

• **A simple experiment** – grow two beans, or two lots of cress, but leave one in the light and one in a dark place. What happens to the one in the dark? (Plants need the light from the sun to grow well.)

Prayabout

Make a picture chart showing all the things we enjoy about the sun and warm weather: drying the washing, flowers, fruit, ice-cream, paddling pools, summer clothes, seaside holidays, etc. Perhaps add one picture each day, and say thank you to God for the sun, and the light and warmth it gives to the earth.

Walkabout

• **In summer,** look out for people enjoying the sun in different ways – eating ice-cream or lollies, playing in paddling pools, eating outside, wearing light summer clothing and sunglasses etc. Look at gardens to see flowers with their petals open to the sun. Look for shadows, and see how they change at different times of day.

• **In autumn,** look for fruit ripening on trees. Explain that the warmth of the sun makes the fruit ripe – soft and sweet – and often changes the colour of the skin too.

• **In winter,** look in a travel agent's windows or brochures to see all the sunny places. Notice that even when it's bright and sunny in winter it's often still cold. Small children don't realise this instinctively – mine always wanted me to fill the paddling pool whenever it was sunny, regardless of the date or the temperature!

• **In spring,** watch for the first signs of the earth warming up after the winter – snowdrops and crocuses, daffodils and forsythia, the trees coming into leaf.

• **Look for sundials** – in gardens of old houses, on church towers, in some public places – and for awnings over shops and cafes – used to protect from too much sun.

COLD WEATHER

Talkabout

• **Snowflakes.** Try to find a book with photos or pictures of magnified snowflakes. Point out that every single snowflake is different.

• **Frost on the ground and in the air;** if you have a room cold enough, let your child see frost patterns on a window next time 'Jack Frost' is about.

• **Find some books with pictures of cold countries.** What do people wear and live in? Why are polar bears white?

Readabout

There are lots of story books for children about snow and cold weather. You probably know some of the following:

• *Postman Pat Goes Sledging* by John Cunliffe (André Deutsch, ISBN 0 233 97676 0)

• *Snow in the Dark Wood* by Peggy Blakeley (A and C Black, ISBN 0 7136 2356 X)

• *The Big Snowstorm* by Hans Peterson (Burke, ISBN 0 222 00490 8)

• *Topsy and Tim's Snowy Day* by Jean and Gareth Anderson (Blackie)

• *Brenda Helps Grandmother* by Astrid Lindgren (Burke, ISBN 0 222 69155 7)

• *Little Grey Rabbit's Christmas* by Alison Uttley (Collins, ISBN 0 00 194289 1). (If you can find it, an abridged version is better for today's under-fives; if you can't the pictures are lovely to look at with a young child.)

• *The Snowman* by Raymond Briggs (Hamish Hamilton, ISBN 0 241 11797 6)

Walkabout

Next time the weather is cold, **see how many cold weather things you can spot:** ice on puddles, frost on grass, maybe snow, people in cold weather clothes, seeing your breath as you exhale…

Notice what animals and birds do when it's cold.

Howabout

• **Cutting out snowflakes** from circles of paper and sticking them on a window or dark background.

• **Feeding the birds in cold weather.**

Prayabout

Make a cold weather picture to which you add a little each day. Use a black piece of paper and put on it the outline of eg a snowman, icicles, trees and houses, and a pond. Let your child stick on cotton wool for snow, glitter for ice and frost, and draw in more snow with chalk. Each day thank God for cold weather – and warm homes.

WEATHER
RAIN

Talkabout
- **Rain and clouds, thunder and lightning.**
- **How do we know it's going to rain?**
- **Where does all the water go?**
- **What happens if we don't get enough rain? If we get too much?**

Readabout
- *Postman Pat's Rainy Day* by John Cunliffe (Andre Deutsch).
- *Mr McNally's Hat* – another story about the lovable Alfie – in *The Big Alfie and Annie Rose Storybook* by Shirley Hughes, found in several different editions.
- *A Walk in the Rain* by Rosemary Border (Macdonald).
- 'Wet' – one of many lovely poems about a young child's everyday experiences, right through the year, in *Out and About* by Shirley Hughes (Walker Books).

Walkabout
Why not go out in the rain and really enjoy it? For adults rain has mostly nuisance value, unless we're keen gardeners, but for young children it's fun! They want to go out in the rain. So next time it pours, unless it's bitterly cold, go out with your children and enjoy it! Let them splash as much as they like in the puddles; watch the ducks, see the water running into the drains in the gutter (where does it go?), smell the freshness after the rain; look at the raindrops on trees and hedges. If you can resign yourself to the fact that you will need a complete change of clothes each, you may even find you have fun too!

Howabout
Making a weather chart. Make a chart for a week or a fortnight, with the days of the week, and a space to draw a cloud and raindrops every time it rains, or make a permanent weather chart from two large circles of cardboard (eg from a cereal packet). Divide one circle into six equal sections and draw a picture of a different sort of weather in each – rainy, sunny, cloudy, windy, foggy, snowy. From the top circle cut out a one-sixth section, and join the two circles with a brass paper-fastener; add a piece of thread to hang it up, and then each day you can display the day's weather.

Prayabout
Make a simple rain mobile with cut-outs of rainclouds, rainbows, umbrellas and wellingtons, hung by threads from a wire coat-hanger. Thank God for the rain every day this week.

WEATHER
WIND & AIR

Talkabout
- **The air** is something we take for granted and it's easy to forget that things that seem obvious to us (like if you let go of your balloon outside on a breezy day it will blow away) have to be learnt by a small child. There are lots of everyday activities that involve the air or the wind, and you can increase your child's understanding and vocabulary by talking about them to her.
- Point out **the wind** blowing the trees; we can't see the wind itself but we can feel it and hear it (what sort of noise?) and see what it does.
- You could perhaps **find some poems about the wind** in a library book, or look at pictures of hot air balloons, hang-gliders, wind-surfing and parachutes, as well as of boats with sails.

Readabout
- Look for *The Wind Blew* by Pat Hutchins and *Mrs Mopple's Washing Day*.
- *The Blue Balloon* by Mick Inkpen (Hodder and Stoughton, ISBN 0 340 50125 1).

Walkabout
- **As you go about this week be on the lookout for things connected with the wind or air,** eg seeing washing blowing on a washing line, looking for the air point at the garage, looking for kites or balloons, or wind-powered models in gardens.
- Some older shops and restaurants still have fans, and a hairdresser uses warm air from a hair dryer to dry people's hair.
- If you happen to live near a windmill it would be worth a visit.
- Some confectionery has air bubbles – Wispa, Aero, Crunchie, for example.

Howabout
- **Finding a bicycle pump and letting your child feel the air coming from it.**
- **Blowing bubbles.**
- **Looking for air-borne seeds** like dandelion clocks and sycamore 'wings'.
- **Doing an experiment** to show that candle flames need air to burn. Light a candle and put a jam jar over the top; the flame will rapidly die.
- **Blowing up a balloon and then letting it go** without tying the end; watch and hear the air coming out of it.
- **Letting your child feel the air going into her lungs,** which are something like two big balloons to be filled with air. What happens if she's been running a lot?
- **Blowing air with a straw into a jam jar half-filled with water;** what does the air make? How do fish breathe? How do whales and dolphins breathe? How do divers like people who work under water get their air?

Prayabout
Make a poster with a big bunch of seven balloons – either drawn or cut out of coloured paper. Each day draw or write on a balloon something you've seen the wind or air do on that day, and thank God for air.

CHRISTMAS: 1
THE ANNUNCIATION

Talkabout

• **Messages:** what messages have you received recently? Were they good or bad news?

• **Postmen, stamps, letters** sent abroad by airmail. Show your child a postmark on a letter.

• **Talk about the story of the angel** telling Mary that she would bear Jesus, and perhaps find a picture of it in a children's Bible story book.

• **Christmas cards** – special messages sent to friends at Christmas.

Readabout

Postman Pat Takes a Message by John Cunliffe (André Deutsch).

Walkabout

• As you go out this week, **look at post boxes and telephone kiosks.** What colour are they? Look for phones in big shops. Look at people's letterboxes – are any difficult for the postman? How many mail vans can you see? Have you ever watched a postman emptying a post box?

• **Read other 'messages' in shop windows,** such as 'For sale' notices.

Howabout

• **Beginning a Christmas scrapbook** with your child: put into it pictures from old Christmas cards showing the Christmas story, scraps of wrapping paper, tinsel, Christmas ribbon etc. Let your child do as much as possible himself.

• **Making an Advent wreath.** You can buy a polystyrene ring with four candleholders in it from a florist; wind evergreens round the ring and add four red, white or gold candles, perhaps with some small pine cones or beech cups sprayed silver or gold. Light one candle four Sundays before Christmas, two candles three Sundays before and so on. A cheaper version can be made by covering four large potatoes in aluminium foil, putting them close together on a plate or small tray, and buying four candle holders designed for flower arranging, one for each potato. Decorate with greenery as above, anchoring it in place with hair pins if necessary.

• **Helping your child make some Christmas cards for special people.**

Prayabout

Use the Ladybird book *Baby Jesus* as a focus for your prayers this week and throughout the pre-Christmas period. Perhaps read only the part of the story relevant to each week's theme, remembering that small children love repetition. Then thank God together for the fun and anticipation of Christmas.

CHRISTMAS: 2
THE JOURNEY

Talkabout

• **Babies** – show your child her baby pictures and any baby toys or mementoes you still have. Talk of the excitement and joy of a new baby, and how special she was and still is to you.

• **Journeys** (Mary and Joseph went on a journey to Bethlehem) – are you going away at Christmas? How will you travel? In some parts of the world people still travel on foot, or by donkey or camel.

Walkabout

As you are out this week, **look for babies!** Look at baby clothes and equipment in shops – much more than Mary would have had for baby Jesus.

Howabout

• **Making a baby poster,** using pictures of babies from catalogues and advertisements?

• **Making a crib scene at home.** It can be as simple or as elaborate as you have time and energy for. Use an old shoebox for the stable, perhaps covered with wallpaper outside. Put straw on the floor, make a manger from Plasticine or a matchbox. If you have toy farm figures you could use those figures in the crib, or make some from kitchen paper rolls. Cover them in scraps of cloth, add faces in felt-tip pen, and head-dresses held with rubber bands.

Prayabout

Continue reading the Christmas story with your child: if you have made a crib, use it as a focus as you thank God for Christmas. Sing 'Away in a manger'.

CHRISTMAS: 3
THE SHEPHERDS

Talkabout

• **Sheep and shepherds, wool and woollen clothes, spinning and weaving.** We wear wool to keep us warm, so lots of winter clothes have wool in them.

Readabout

• **Re-read any favourite stories** about sheep, eg many of the Postman Pat stories feature sheep, or borrow from the library a beautifully illustrated story for young children called *The Shepherd Boy* by Kim Lewis (Walker Books, ISBN 0 7445 1502 5).

• *Angel Mae* by Shirley Hughes (Walker Books, ISBN 0 7445 1136 4), an enchanting story of a small girl in a nativity play and the birth of her baby sister.

Walkabout

As you go about this week, **look for woollen clothes, at wool in wool shops – lots of lovely colours – and for pictures of sheep.** You could also see if you can spot angels in Christmas displays in shops and streets. If you live in the country, try to see some sheep.

Howabout

• **Adding sheep, shepherds and angels to your crib scene.**

• **Making a simple Christmas mobile:** cut out pictures/shapes of an angel, Mary, a manger, a baby, a shepherd and a sheep, and suspend them from a wire coat hanger (cover the sharp end of the hook).

Prayabout

Use this prayer with your child this week:

'Dear God, thank you for sending Jesus into the world. Help us to love him and follow him all our lives. Amen.'

CHRISTMAS: 4
THE WISE MEN

Talkabout

• **Stars** – and take your child out to look at them.

• **Lights** – how many different kinds have you got in your house? How do they work? What do you do if there's a power cut? (Emphasise again that it's very dangerous to touch plugs and lights.)

• **Talk about the wise men** – how did they travel? Probably on camels. Because they brought gifts to Jesus, who was God's gift to us, we give other people gifts at Christmas time.

Readabout

Children of four upwards would probably enjoy the story of Baboushka, especially in the Lion edition (ISBN 0 85648 407 5) which tells the story very simply with lovely bright illustrations and words and music for the Baboushka carol.

Walkabout

How many lights can you see this week? Street lights of different kinds, illuminated signs, house lights, traffic lights, Christmas lights and decorations…

Howabout

• **Making some Christmas tree gifts/decorations.** Buy a pack of mini-boxes of Smarties or raisins, and help your child to wrap them in shiny Christmas paper with a loop of ribbon or metallic thread to hang them on the tree. If you want them to be permanent decorations use empty matchboxes.

• **Adding the wise men and maybe camels** (use two egg box sections for humps and pipe cleaners for legs) to your crib scene.

Prayabout

• **Make a Christingle for your child** or maybe one for each member of the family. You could use this prayer:

Father God,
thank you for these Christingles.
They remind us
of your love and goodness.
They remind us
that you sent Jesus to be a light.
Help us to love you
and to love others as he did.
Amen.

• As you pray this week, **focus on some of the preparations for Christmas** – decorations, lights, the tree, special food, presents. Perhaps stand and look at them (one each day) as you pray this prayer:

Lord Jesus, thank you for
the fun of getting ready for Christmas.
Thank you for this/these…
Thank you for coming as a baby
at Christmas time. Amen.

CAROL SERVICE

Readabout

Take some time to think about the events of the first Christmas.

Read the story of the birth of Jesus in a modern version of the Bible, or use one of the many excellent books on the market such as *The Lion Book of Bible Stories and Prayers*. Sing some simple carols together.

Howabout

• **Remembering Jesus as the light of the world.**

• Pushing a candle into the centre of some oasis and surround it with holly, ivy, small glass baubles, dried flowers etc. **Light the candle on Christmas Day and remember Jesus.**

• **Baking a birthday cake for Jesus.** Your child will enjoy helping to bake and decorate a simple sponge cake. Silver balls are festive and, if you can, pipe the words Happy Birthday Jesus on the top.

Prayabout

Create space for Jesus. Place the birthday cards you made in a prominent place and make a small flower arrangement to go alongside them. Use it as a focus for the real meaning of Christmas.

PALM SUNDAY

Talkabout

• **The reasons why the people threw their cloaks down on the ground** (it was a sign of royalty, as was the waving of branches).

• **The cross on a donkey's back.** Next time you see a donkey, look for the darker markings in the hair.

Readabout

'Pussy willow time' in *Haffertee's First Easter* by Janet and John Perkins (Lion).

Howabout

• **Making a collage donkey** out of scraps of grey material, or use the one you made at church. Put your collage of Jesus on a donkey in a special place in your house, with a palm cross, if your church gives them out, and a stony road of some smooth, clean stones from the garden.

• **Finding out about the events of Holy Week** from a children's story Bible or one of the Gospels. (See Luke 19:28–48 and chapters 22 and 23.)

• If you have any Jewish friends, ask them to tell you about their **Passover celebrations**, or find a book from your library.

Prayabout

Help your child make their own prayer picture of Jesus going into Jerusalem, using brown paint for the road and palm prints for the palm branches. Help them to write 'Hooray for Jesus!' underneath.

FESTIVAL SERVICES
GOOD FRIDAY

Readabout

• *Haffertee's First Easter* by Janet and John Perkins (Lion). Haffertee discovers all about pancakes, Easter eggs and Mr Jesus King. The chapter 'Pieces of Howl' is especially relevant to Good Friday.

• *Grandpa and Me* by Marlee and Benny Alex (Lion) is a heartwarming book about a small girl's relationship with her grandad. It sensitively faces the issues of death and dying when first a kitten and then Grandpa dies. An excellent book to introduce young children to the concept of death.

Howabout

• **Eating some hot cross buns together** and remembering the significance of the cross on them.

• **Singing**

Hot cross buns,
Hot cross buns.
One a penny, two a penny,
Hot cross buns.

•**Making an Easter garden** with your child, to be finished off on Easter day. Fill an old tray, or toffee tin, with earth and shape a hill at one end and a tomb at the other. Make paths from small stones. Add three crosses on the hill, made from twigs. Stick dead twigs into the garden to make it look sad and lonely.

On Easter day, decorate it with lots of colourful flowers, and move the stone from the front of the tomb.

Prayabout

Think about being lonely and afraid and remember that Jesus is always there. **Say a prayer at bed-time for anyone you know who may be lonely and afraid tonight.**

FESTIVAL SERVICES
EASTER

Talkabout

Being sad and happy. What things make your child happy and sad? What other feelings does s/he have? When?

(Many adults find it hard to talk about their feelings, and children are quick to realise this. Consequently they grow up finding it hard to talk about feelings, too!) Try experimenting together by saying, 'Right now I feel.... happy/sad/cold/tired/cross etc,' and let your child discover ways of describing all sorts of feelings.

Readabout

• *Haffertee's First Easter* by Janet and John Perkins (Lion) describes how this little soft toy hamster discovers all about Mr Jesus King and the events that lead up to Easter Day.

• *Goose Lays an Egg* by Helen Piers (Methuen) follows the difficulties of Goose as she tries to find a suitable place for her nest. She finally lays her eggs in a very unusual place indeed!

Walkabout

Look in gardens and parks for trees and shrubs breaking into leaf. Which ones are fully out? Which ones are not out at all? Do any trees or shrubs flower before they get their leaves?

Howabout

Having an Easter egg hunt. You could use chocolate eggs or real, decorated boiled eggs. You can turn white eggs into coloured ones by hard-boiling them in a strong solution of cake colouring or vegetable dye. Try doing it by wrapping onion skins or spinach leaves round them. Secure the leaves by wrapping a piece of material round the egg and fastening it with string or a rubber band.

Prayabout

• **Make a visual prayer with your child, about spring.** Use a small shelf or surface. Cover it with a cloth or some bright material (yellow or green works well). Collect some flowers, budding twigs, pussy willow etc and perhaps add some clean empty egg shells too. If you wish you could find some pictures of baby animals – lambs, chicks – and display them as well. Remind your child that God makes all these things grow in the spring. Say a short prayer together, or put up the words, 'My God is so BIG!'

• For more Easter and spring activities see *The Spring Activity Book* (Lion).

PENTECOST (Whitsun)

Walkabout

The Bible sometimes describes God the Holy Spirit as a 'rushing wind'. So next time it's a windy day, **go for a walk in the wind**. Perhaps you have a kite you could fly too.

Howabout

- **Finding out about the wind and air.** Try this experiment to show there is air in a jar. Place a candle firmly on a saucer and fill the saucer with water. Light the candle and then carefully place a large upturned jam jar on the saucer. After a few seconds the candle will go out (because all the oxygen has been used up) and some water will be sucked up into the jar (to take its place). AMAZING!

- **Making and sending a card to a friend** to show you are thinking about them?

- **Keeping a chart for a week to show how windy it has been?** Help your child to decorate a piece of paper then list the days of the week down one side. Make (or draw on) little trees, bent over by the wind, to show how windy it is. Stick on one tree if it isn't very windy, lots of trees if it is!

Prayabout

Another Biblical symbol for the Holy Spirit is the dove. **Make some more doves** to remind you that God is always with you. Hang them on an old coat hanger and suspend it where the air will move the doves. Some suitable prayers can be found in *The Lion Book of Children's Prayers*.

HELP!

Advice is available from many sources

SOCIAL SERVICES

If you want to set up a playgroup for under-fives, you **must** contact the Social Services Department of your local authority, as there is a legal requirement for all playgroups to be registered with them. Certain basic conditions must be met, eg the number of toilets and washing facilities, but requirements vary from one authority to another. Most produce a booklet which outlines their particular regulations. Social Services Departments usually have a day-care advisor with specialist knowledge of the needs of under-fives who will generally visit and advise in the early stages of setting up a playgroup. She will also know about all sorts of other facilities such as toy libraries, training courses and where to obtain equipment, and even grants!

If you are setting up a group other than a playgroup, there is no legal requirement to inform Social Services, but it could be worth contacting them as they may well be able to help you. You can find the address and telephone number in your local directory or Yellow Pages, often under 'County Council' or 'Borough Council'.

PRE-SCHOOL PLAYGROUPS ASSOCIATION

This is the foremost voluntary agency for under-fives in England, and there are separate associations for other parts of the UK. There are member groups in thirty-three other countries. They have a wealth of expertise and many parent and toddler groups as well as playgroups are affiliated to them. They offer an excellent group insurance package and publish a very useful catalogue. For an information pack, write to • **The Information Centre, PPA National Centre,** 61-63 Kings Cross Road, London WC1X 9LL, tel: 071 833 0991.

PUBLIC LIBRARY SERVICE

Do use your library! Some local authority library services publish lists of books suitable for pre-school children, often classified into categories – fun with letters, developing imagination etc. It's worth getting hold of anything like this for basic reference. Some libraries are happy to send a computer print-out of books available on a particular topic – musical instruments for example. Some authorities have a children's librarian who may be available to help and advise if you have enough money to buy some books. Ask at your local library initially.

CHURCH PASTORAL AID SOCIETY

This organisation has a whole department geared to Ministry Among Women, headed by Kathryn Pritchard, with a regular news magazine, *Connect*, which gives details of local events and regional representatives. As its name suggests MAW is concerned for all aspects of church life involving women, including groups for under-fives, and they have some useful publications. It would be worth adding your name to their mailing list. Write for details to • Miss Sue Cartwright, Admin. Sec., **CPAS Ministry Among Women,** Athena Drive, Tachbrook Park, Warwick CV34 6NG.

SCRIPTURE UNION

SU has been working with children and families in and outside church situations for more than a century. Its Education in Churches department has experienced staff who could advise you or point you to publications that would help. Write to • **SU House,** 130 City Road, London EC1V 2NJ. For information on Scripture Union's family work contact Joan King at • **The Scripture Union Training Centre,** 26-30 Heathcoat Street, Nottingham NG1 3AA.

BOOKS

Two books which will help you think about work with children and develop appropriate skills are:
• *Children Finding Faith* by Francis Bridger (Scripture Union, 1988, ISBN 0 86201 460 3),
• *Under-Fives Welcome!* by Kathleen Crawford (Scripture Union, 1990, ISBN 0 86201 559 6).

DENOMINATIONAL STAFF

Each Anglican diocese in England has a children's diocesan oficer, who would also be able to advise on many aspects of running a group. Ask your vicar or at the local library for the contact point. Other denominations will also have specialist advisers on work with young children. Contact your denominational headquarters.

SUPPLIES AND EQUIPMENT

Early Learning Centres have an excellent range of 'own brand' equipment such as chunky paint-brushes, non-spill paint pots, large containers of glue which can be decanted into yoghurt pots etc. They also publish a comprehensive catalogue and offer a mail order service: write to • **Early Learning Centre,** South Marston, Swindon SN3 4TJ.

A large department store with a good toy section may be the best place to buy basics like paint, brushes, PVA glue ('school' glue), scissors and so on. If neither of these options is available, **PPA local branches** often operate a 'shop' say once a month or twice a term, where basic supplies, bought in bulk at a discount, are offered to affiliated groups, again at very competitive prices.

If all these are impossible, you may have to order from one of the educational suppliers – excellent quality but with prices to match! It's worth obtaining some catalogues to give you an idea of their prices, and if you want large equipment, like a climbing frame, look at what they have to offer.

• **James Galt and Company Ltd.,** Brookfield Road, Cheadle, Cheshire SK8 2PN.

• **Hestair Hope Education,** St Philips Drive, Royton, Oldham OL2 6AG.

• **Nottingham Educational Supplies,** Ludlow Hill Road, West Bridgford, Nottingham NG2 6HD.

PAPER, CARD, ETC

For colouring and drawing, the cheapest paper is newsprint, often available from a local newspaper, which will sell off ends of rolls when it's no longer economic to use the roll for printing. The advantage is that it is very cheap; the disadvantages are that the rolls are very heavy and bulky so storage can be a problem, and the paper itself is very thin and easily torn, and unsuitable for paint. Not all newspapers sell their roll ends, but it's worth enquiring by ringing your local paper. They are usually very helpful. If newsprint is not available, a fairly cheap alternative is a roll of decorators' lining paper for activities requiring crayons or pencils.

Used computer paper is ideal for drawing but less good for gluing or paint, though better than newsprint or lining paper.

Printers and Stationers (see Yellow Pages) may also be worth contacting for rather better quality paper. You may be able to buy reams of 'all purpose' paper at comparatively low cost or, better still, off-cuts. A friendly local printer would probably be glad to let you have them if you explain what you want them for. Especially useful are off-cuts of card, normally a very expensive commodity, which can be used for a variety of craft activities.

For many activities and for some displays you need sugar paper. Your local PPA may help but if not it might be worth contacting your local primary school to find out if they know of a source of paper, card offcuts etc. They may know local suppliers who would help by providing small mixed packs of coloured paper which could only otherwise be bought in unmanageable quantities from larger suppliers. You may be able to join forces with another local group to buy in bulk – even if you have to store things under beds!

Finally, ask in **wallpaper shops** for their out of date wallpaper sample books which can be used for all sorts of things.

USEFUL 'SCRAP'

The Federation of Resource Centres collects industrial 'scrap' and reissues it for use in voluntary charitable groups. Subscriber groups typically pay an annual affiliation fee and receive scrap free. Contact Lin Thurston, 25 Bullivant Stret, St Anns, Nottingham, tel: 0242 221700, for centres in northern England. Registered contacts are:

• **South East:** Jane Skead and Helen Moore, South London Childrens Scrap Scheme, The Spike, Consort Road, London SE15, tel: 071 277 5953.

• **South West:** Pete Melvey, Community Development Division, DLTA, Civic Centre, Southampton SO9 4XF, tel: 0703 832267.

• **Midlands:** Polly Howells, Rushcliffe Play Forum, 75 Raleigh Street, Nottingham NG7 4DL, tel: 0602 788080.

• **Scotland:** Margaret Miller, Glasgow Playschemes Asociation, 140 Wallace Street, Glasgow G5 8EQ, tel: 041 425 7577.